# THEY SHALL NOT HURT

# THEY SHALL NOT HURT

## Human Suffering and Human Caring

Edited by

Rodney L. Taylor and Jean Watson

COLORADO ASSOCIATED UNIVERSITY PRESS

Colorado Associated University Press is a cooperative publishing enterprise supported, in part, by Adams State College, Colorado State University, Fort Lewis College, Mesa State College, Metropolitan State College,
University of Colorado, University of Northern Colorado, University of
Southern Colorado, and Western State College.

The paper used in this publication meets the minimum requirements of
American National Standard for Information Sciences—Permanence of
Paper for Printed Library Materials. ANSI Z39.48–1984

**Library of Congress Cataloging-in-Publication Data**

They shall not hurt.

  Includes bibliographies.
  1. Suffering — Religious aspects. 2. Suffering.
3. Caring. 4. Medical ethics. I. Taylor, Rodney Leon,
1944-      . II. Watson, Jean, 1940-      .
BL65.S85T48 1989      128'.4      89-904
ISBN 0-87081-201-7
ISBN 0-87081-203-3 (pbk.)

"Compassion: A Critique of Moral Rationalism," by William J. Prior, is
reprinted by permission of *Philosophy Theology:* Marquette University
Quarterly.

"Tulips" Copyright ©1962 by Ted Hughes. From THE COLLECTED
POEMS OF SYLVIA PLATH by Sylvia Plath. Reprinted by permission
of Harper & Row, Publishers, Inc.

# Contents

# Editors

Rodney L. Taylor, Ph.D., Associate Dean of the Graduate School and Professor of Religious Studies, University of Colorado at Boulder

Jean Watson, R.N., Ph.D., F.A.A.N., Professor and Dean, School of Nursing, Director, Center for Human Caring, University of Colorado Health Sciences Center, Denver

# Contributors

Frederick R. Abrams, M.D., Director, The Center for Applied Biomedical Ethics, Rose Medical Center, Denver

Carole Anderson, R.N., Ph.D., F.A.A.N., Dean, School of Nursing, Ohio State University

David Little, Ph.D., Professor of Comparative Ethics, University of Virginia, Jennings Randolph Distinguished Fellow, United States Institute of Peace, Washington D.C.

Nel Noddings, Ph.D., Professor of Ethics, School of Education, Standford University

William Prior, Ph.D., Associate Professor of Philosophy, University of Santa Clara

RODNEY L. TAYLOR and JEAN WATSON

# Introduction

We begin with the all too common truism that humankind suffers. Suffering, psychological or physical, is universal in scope. It often seems that the level of suffering is what, tragically, determines the quality of human existence. There is nothing new in this observation. Eastern and Western cultures alike have frequently expressed the ubiquity of suffering and have sought various means to articulate the state of suffering, to explicate its causes, and to remedy its destructive effects. The benefits of modern technological society have not eradicated human suffering; in certain ways they seem only to have exacerbated it. To invent a tool is not necessarily to solve a problem. Human suffering is a deep and complex problem intimately and intricately related to the very nature of human existence.

With modern tools we have created specialized fields of knowledge, seeking the profoundest understanding of the inner workings of nature and human life. Our pedagogy has compartmentalized our knowledge, and our modern university is the epitome of educational theory. The result, as we are well aware, is indeed specialized knowledge—extraordinarily specialized! Specialization has made possible a deep penetration into various features of human existence, but it has also created something of a paradox. With increased specialization has come the inability to explore the dimensions of human life conjointly with others. Each specialized area is a culture unto itself. It has its particular worldview, its methodology; it has its own language; it has even its own artifacts and history—a set of tools and the development of those tools.

1

This, too, is not a new or earth-shaking perception. It has been commented on in many contexts and described as the plight of the modern educational institution. Attempts have been made to remedy it; to structure curricula to be broadly inclusive of different fields, different approaches, different languages if you will; to permit us to develop broad concerns and sensitivities, so that our understanding of the human condition will encompass the variety and range of experiences that contribute to the commonality of human life.

There is still the need to address a more basic level—the individual—to put the work of the individual scholar in its largest context. All too often, we must begin by simply reminding scholars that their specialized field of research, no matter how specialized, does have relevancy to the human condition. How frequently this is simply forgotten. The Taoist philosopher Chuang Tzu wrote, more than two thousand years ago, that you cannot discuss the sea with a frog in a well, he is cramped by the confines he lives in; and you cannnot discuss the Way with a scholar, he is cramped by a head full of ideas!

It is difficult enough simply to communicate across disciplinary lines within common colleges. In the humanities, there is little occasion for philosophers, historians, or specialists in English literature or religion to share perspectives, even though it is clear that workers in all these fields are probing the human condition. There are barriers, primarily methodological and theoretical, that prevent sharing or even recognizing the common pursuit. This is equally true of the social sciences and the natural sciences. It is, of course, even more true when we attempt to bridge the gap between each area. Attempts at genuine cross-disciplinary work are few and far between. When we add the medical and caring professions, it is very rare to see any attempt to cross over, to engage in cross-disciplinary study, or even to admit that there are common issues at stake.

The unique task of this book is to explore a new horizon—the context within which the humanities and the professions of human caring intersect and interact. This is not simply an attempt to bridge the gaps in the disciplines of the humanities or even to try to chart common ground among the humanities, social sciences, and natural sciences. This is an attempt to span a far-reaching expanse, where few would even think of commonalities. From the beginning, our assumption has been that there is common ground. Those in the humanities are deeply committed to understanding the human condition. Such understanding arises from the study of that condition in the context of world cultures, and the articulation of individual attempts to seek self-understanding through literary, philosophical, religious, or artistic modes. In turn, those in the health and caring professions are equally committed to understanding the human condition in order to remedy and transform it by applying scientific knowledge through specific technologies.

The commonality is the human condition, but not simply the human condition. It is the human condition fraught with suffering that has been, we might say, the primary motivation for self-understanding and self-transformation. In an important sense, then, human suffering is central to the ways in which the various disciplines have sought self-understanding and self-transformation.

In bringing these differing perspectives to bear on the question of suffering, we have found, even in this pioneering effort, that the humanities and the health and human-caring professions are reciprocal and ultimately interdependent.

The health and human-caring sciences have been dominated by instructional programs in scientific and technological knowledge. This focus has been at the expense of attention to values, ethics, and the inner complexity of patients' subjective experiences. It needs to be recognized that patients' feelings, values, and personal meanings—their own self-understanding—can be critical to the reestablishment of health, and thus to the processes of human caring. The history of the health and human-caring sciences indicates clearly that little attention has been given to these areas in professional training. Even a small curricular emphasis on humanitarian subject matter and, by extension, the humanities, has suffered grievously from impoverished instructional strategies. The benefit of introducing the humanities into the health and human-caring sciences is that it provides strategies for approaching the questions of human wholeness and of fulfilling the human needs of the patient.

The humanities, in turn, have been dominated by pedagogical models that have focused on specific forms of method and theory, issues of language study, historical study, and textual or hermeneutical meanings. This has produced technical and sophisticated knowledge in the various fields of the humanities. What has not been present to any large degree is what is often rather disparagingly referred to as "applied humanities"; that is, the attempt to relate the traditions of human self-expression to real problems and real people in the world—in a sense, to see the relevancy of what humanities scholars study. In some part, this book is precisely directed to this area; we suggest that humanities scholars can and perhaps should bring their expertise to bear on real people and real problems. This is the bridge between the humanities and what is humane and humanitarian.

The chapters in this book attempt to show specific areas of expertise coming both from the humanities and the health and human-caring sciences, but they also focus on the common problem of human suffering. Each chapter lends its own articulation to the ways human suffering has been stated and explained, and the manner in which its rectification has been sought.

This book begins with the humanities perspective—Eastern, Western, and comparative—with chapters by Rodney L. Taylor, William Prior, and David Little. Taylor's chapter, "Compassion, Caring, and the Religious Response to Suffering," outlines the importance of suffering to general religious responses to the world. Suffering is not something to be discarded by religious traditions. In fact, it is seen as central to the task of giving meaning to the world. A religious worldview claims there is meaning and purpose in the world. As there is suffering, it too must be given a role in that meaning and purpose. Taylor focuses on classical Eastern religious responses to suffering. Hindu and Buddhist responses generally deny the ultimate reality of suffering, though they allow conditional status for the afflicted. The Confucian response accepts suffering as a given. In general, it is clear that there are strategies to give meaning to suffering. In turn, different religious traditions have different understandings of the meaning of suffering—a telling complexity for the health-care professional dealing with the religious sensitivities of the patient.

William Prior's chapter, "Compassion: A Critique of Moral Rationalism," focuses on the character of compassion as a natural human sentiment; that is, natural in a normative and evaluative sense. Compassion is the natural response to suffering, a feeling most of us would share. Prior goes on to argue, however, that while most of us would agree that compassion is a response natural to human nature (an argument shared with the Confucian perspective argued by Taylor), Western moral philosophers have tended to associate compassion almost exclusively with rationality. In its connection with rationality, compassion was not given its role as a motivating factor in moral psychology. Prior's chapter applies this general theory to practical issues—specifically the treatment of certain handicapped populations, arguing that where moral rationalism fails in adequate responses, the approach of compassion has specific benefits. Where moral rationalism has placed value on lives, the intrinsic value of the lives of the handicapped, Prior argues that compassion seeks to fill needs. Like the Good Samaritan, compassion requires that we respond to the needs of the person. Here, too, we see the humanities arguing for humaneness, suggesting the complexity of our responses either as human-caring professionals, or as people in a special moral relation to someone who is sick.

Little's chapter, "Human Suffering in Comparative Perspective," attempts to draw our attention to comparative ways in which suffering might be understood. Little begins by pointing out the central role that suffering occupies in both Eastern and Western religious traditions. To the question, why is it that the wicked live prosperously while the innocent seem to suffer so greatly, the Zoroastrian responds by proclaiming a radical dualism of good and evil and a world dominated by the forces of evil. A Christian responds with a model of a sovereign, predestining God. Hinduism and Buddhism suggest the outcomes of previous lifetimes. Even given these differences in response, there is something of commonality, and it is this possible comparative model that Little develops. At the applied level, we begin with the assumption that humans have a conscious and shared experience of intense suffering. At another level, we see that there are four primary types of suffering: retributive, therapeutic, pedagogical, and vicarious. These categories are then applied to Christianity and Buddhism. In Christianity, suffering is at least partially retributive, though there is dissatisfaction with the idea. There is also a strong theme of therapeutic suffering in which the sufferer needs a physician, who is Jesus. Suffering is also seen as instructional. There are elements of Christianity that suggest that Jesus is not only physician, but substitute. Thus, we see also vicarious suffering. These categories also illuminate the Buddhist response to suffering. The point, then, is to draw our attention to the commonality of the experience of suffering and the role it has played in both Eastern and Western religious thought. This suggests not only the universality of suffering, but the potentiality that suffering is what Little calls "a common reference point in human life with its own 'logic.' " While suffering has been thought about in many ways, there is also a certain structure to the ways it has been articulated. Suffering produces certain types of responses; this suggests the importance of applied sensitivities to the ways in which suffering will be met and understood by the person who is suffering.

Noddings' chapter, "Woman's Answer to Job," takes us from the purview of the humanities to a social-scientific view of both the humanities and the health and human-caring sciences. Noddings challenges traditional perspectives, arguing that there is an answer to Job. It is not to accept the redemptive features of one's own suffering, whether retributive, therapeutic, pedagogical, or vicarious. It is to see that suffering has a cause or a number of causes but does not have to be accepted as part of the meaning of the universe. In addition, Noddings challenges the traditional male-dominated models of interpretation, substituting an ethics of caring for an ethics of justice, by suggesting that woman is in a unique role to offer care to the suffering because of her unique capacity to show caring. Caring, from Noddings' perspective, is a "yearning for the good," a commitment to the reintegration of the person and of humanity as a whole. Nodding argues the importance of the humanities to education in the caring professions primarily as a method to approach the modalities of the patient.

Abrams' chapter, "Medical-Ethical Perspectives on Human Suffering," calls our attention to the practical issues of ethics facing the medical practitioners. Abrams draws a distinction between pain and suffering, suggesting that the physician must be as concerned to eliminate suffering—the psychological response of the individual—as he is to relieve pain—a specifically physiological phenomenon. The aim of medical practice remains healing, but it must necessarily be qualified by the need to ameliorate suffering. Abrams considers several specific areas of suffering. One is simple truth-telling; frequently, the truth about an illness is not shared with the patient. Abrams says, "Suffering can be relieved, by not abandoning the patient when science fails. Although no more can be done against the disease, much more can be done for the patient. Truth-telling relieves the sufferer of uncertainty and mistrust . . . and emphasizes caring in the face of an unpleasant truth." There is also the necessity to recognize the rights of the patient. "Physicians must always be patient advocates." This involves questions of autonomy and consent, and the importance of individual values and religious systems. As advocate of the patient, the physician must take these factors into consideration. Clearly, the responsibility is to see the relation between healing and the lessening of suffering maximized, and also to recognize the dimensions of suffering that permit the physician to remain a patient advocate, appreciating the patient as a whole and subjective being. This, in turn, has important ramifications for the relation of the caring professions to the arts and humanities. Many of the issues most central to Abrams' argument on the rights of the patient are formulated also in the subject matter of the arts and humanities—questions, for example, of the nature of the self and its relation to the world. Whether these be philosophical, religious, literary, or artistic representations of the self, Abrams' suggests that patients be given the right to exercise their values in ways that are meaningful to them, thus recognizing that the integrity of the individual is central, and critical to the goal of healing and eliminating suffering.

Anderson's chapter, "The Severely Physically Disabled: A Subjective Account of Suffering," brings us face to face with the sufferings of the handicapped. Anderson considers the Rehabilitation Act of 1973 and the adoption, in 1975, of the Declaration of Rights of Disabled Persons. As Anderson says, such documents "are testimony to the devalued, discriminated, and prejudiced status of physically disabled persons. Were this not the case, there would not have been the need for such declarations, resolutions, and laws." She focuses on the plight of the physically disabled as a fitting example of suffering. The story is one of a group of disabled and "abled" becoming aware of the tragedy of young disabled persons living in nursing homes, and the attempt to respond to their plight. The limitations of the nursing home are detailed. Anderson relates the attempt to break out of the mold of suffering; to confront, for the first time, the issues of freedom and autonomy;

to break down the barriers of the community and to transcend those barriers, which had appeared to be part of the disability itself.

Anderson's chapter does not let us forget that our issue is, after all, real people and their plight. This is what we need to touch and be able to deal with. This is the common ground of the caring professions and the arts and humanities. As important as theoretical studies are in all these fields, it is when they are focused on the expression of caring that their noblest instincts emerge.

A model for the way in which such instincts can be allowed to emerge and can in fact become a dominant paradigm for movement toward the closest understanding of these fields as they relate to human suffering is provided in the last chapter, by Watson. Watson constructs a model for caring informed by and indebted to the arts and humanities as they express their capacity for humaneness. The goal Watson sets for the future is the development "of a new paradigm that weaves together human caring, arts, and humanities for its new healing possibilities beyond objective science as we seek to understand our human center and our individual lived world—be it suffering or joy." Watson sees parallels between the caring professions and the arts and humanities that are only waiting to be fully expressed and developed. Caring is seen as the fulfillment of a moral ideal—the quest for the good, a moral commitment to the reintegration of humanity. In turn, the arts and humanities may be said to share in this process of reintegration of humanity pursuing a fundamental vision of the wholeness of humanity and the necessity to realize such wholeness, measured in the degree to which the humanities exercise their capacity for humaneness. The response to suffering is a shared response—humanities and human-care alike. It is a measure of the capacity to respond: What Taylor refers to as a religious response to suffering; Prior as a feeling that goes beyond rationality; Little as an experience that has its own logic; Noddings as a yearning for the good; Abrams as patient advocacy; and Anderson as recognizing the inherent suffering in disability. For Watson, it is the quality of subjectivity, the salience of the response of the whole person to other people, measured equally as whole people. The connection ultimately is not simply subjectivity, but intersubjectivity, the capacity to experience the human center.

This is, of course, only one model. Many others might be

possible, and we hope that this book will encourage the creation of other models. Our propose is to demonstrate that there are major commonalities stretching across what, traditionally, have been rigidly divided fields: the caring and health professions and the arts and humanities. When the focus is the suffering of a single person, this gulf is bridged with a genuine humaneness that speaks to the very center of what makes us human beings.

# Compassion, Caring, and the Religious Response to Suffering

A luminous mountain morning. Mist and fire smoke, sun shafts and dark ravines: a peak of Annapurna poises on soft clouds. In fresh light, to the peeping of baby chickens, we take breakfast in the village tea house, and are under way well before seven. A child dragging bent and useless legs is crawling up the hill outside the village. Nose to the stones, goat dung and muddy trickles, she pulls herself along like a broken cricket. We falter, ashamed of our strong step, and noticing this, she gazes up, clear eyes, without resentment—it seems much worse that she is pretty. In Bengal, GS says stiffly, beggars will break their children's knees to achieve this pitiable effect for business purposes: this is his way of expressing his distress. But the child that lies here at our boots is not a beggar, she is merely a child, sharing in curiosity at tall, white strangers. I long to give her something—a new life?—yet am afraid to tamper with such dignity. And so I smile as best I can, and say "Namas-te!" "Good morning." How absurd! And her voice follows as we go away, a small clear smiling voice—"Namas-te"—a Sanskrit word for greeting and parting that means "I salute you."[1]

Thus, we encounter suffering. The meaning we try to give to such an episode often reflects certain basic religious values, recognized or unrecognized. We respond in a variety of ways. We can say, with GS, what a pitiable state: that through economic ruin people are reduced to presenting themselves in such a fashion. These are the causes; surely some reforms must be carried out to rectify this condition. Then the problem will be solved, the suffering will dis-

11

appear. Or, we can respond as Peter Matthiessen does, feeling the dignity of the little girl as a human life and marveling, in a sense, at her self-expression and her incorporation of her condition into her sense of the meaning of the world.

Of course, we can also cry out, like Job, declaring that the righteous suffer unmercifully. We could conclude that on the basis of suffering alone, little of religious truth or meaning can remain. Yet, in a sense, suffering stands at the very center of a religious response to the world. A religious response is by definition one that strives for meaning and purpose in the nature of the universe. A universe that is merely random and ultimately meaningless is the antithesis of any religious worldview. As the philosopher W. T. Stace has said:

> Religion could survive the discoveries that the sun, not the earth, is the center; that men are descended from simian ancestors; that the earth is hundreds of millions of years old. These discoveries may render out of date some of the details of older theological dogmas, may force their restatement in new intellectual frameworks. But they do not touch the essence of the religious vision itself, which is the faith that there is a plan and purpose in the world, that the world is a moral order, that in the end all things are for the best.[2]

Stace has identified the key issue. There must be a purpose behind events, from the point of view that we call religious. Religion can cope with any astronomy, geology, biology, or physics. What it cannot cope with is an inchoate universe. And here lies the paradox! On the one hand, from a religious point of view, all things are for the best, must be for the best. On the other hand, a number of these things that are supposedly for the best precipitate an inordinate amount of suffering.

The solution to the paradox is to suggest that if the religious worldview is to persist, then suffering must be seen as not unrelated, but always secondary to the meaning and purpose of the universe. Or, more specifically, that suffering cannot form a meaningless component of an otherwise meaningful universe. Suffering bears a direct relation to any projected meaning of the universe and cannot be divorced from it. The social anthropologist Clifford Geertz expresses the essential feature of a religious worldview when he concludes that no matter what the level of suffering, there must still be an acceptance of its ultimate meaningfulness.

> The strange opacity of certain empirical events, the dumb senselessness of intense and inexorable pain, and the enigmatic unaccountability of gross iniquity all raise the uncomfortable suspicion that perhaps the world, and hence man's life in the world, has no genuine order at all—no empirical regularity, no emotional form, no moral coherence. And the religious response to this suspicion is in each case the same: the formulation, by means of symbols, of an image of such a genuine order of the world which will account for, and even celebrate, the perceived ambiguities, puzzles and paradoxes in human experience. The effort is not to deny the undeniable—that there are unexplained events, that life hurts or that rain falls upon the just—but to deny that there are inexplicable events, that life is unendurable and that justice is a mirage.[3]

Contemporary philosophy of religion has frequently posed the issue of the verifiability of claims of religious truth: Essentially, on what grounds and in what ways is a religious claim true? In the now well-known parable of the garden and the gardener, the English philosopher John Wisdom attempted to apply the verifiability principle of the logical positivists to religious language. The parable concerns two people who have returned to a long-neglected garden where there are among the weeds a few vigorous old plants. The two argue as to whether a gardener has attended the garden in their absence, and neither can convince the other. Wisdom's point is that these two contrary reactions are to the same empirical facts. In like manner, the meaningfulness or meaninglessness of the universe may be measured by the same datum. From Wisdom's perspective, it is simply a different *feeling* as to which position is to be accepted.

   Granted that one cannot establish the empirical basis for accepting a religious worldview and its claims of truth, is it possible to establish the criterion (or criteria) by which one might falsify a religious point of view? The issue shifts in this direction with the English philosopher Anthony Flew, who draws our attention to the grounds on which a religious claim might be falsified.

> Now it often seems to people who are not religious as if there was no conceivable event or series of events the occurrence of which would be admitted by sophisticated religious people to be sufficient reason for conceding "There wasn't a God after all" or "God does not really

love us then." Someone tells us that God loves us as a father loves his children. We are reassured. But then we see a child dying of inoperable cancer of the throat. His earthly father is driven frantic in his efforts to help, but his Heavenly father reveals no obvious sign of concern. Some qualification is made—God's love is "not merely human love," or it is "an inscrutable love," perhaps—and we realize that such sufferings are quite compatible with the truth of the assertion that "God loves us as a father (but, of course . . .)." We are reassured again. . . . Just what would have to happen not merely (morally and wrongly) to tempt but also (logically and rightly) to entitle us to say, "God does not love us" or even "God does not exist?" I therefore put . . . the simple central question, "What would have to occur or to have occurred to constitute for you a disproof of the love of, or the existence of, God?"[4]

One possible answer to Flew's question is to suggest that such disproof of a religious claim could be the result of suffering so great that the individual enduring it concludes that there can be no explanation and thus no meaning, no purpose, and no order in the universe. It is the suffering itself that shifts the balance of proof toward the harsh reality of accepting a meaningless universe. The suffering of Job epitomizes the individual's tenacity in the face of seeming irrational suffering. Job's friends attempt to convince him that the reason for his suffering lies in some offense he has committed and is thus a punishment wrought on him, but Job maintains his own righteousness and innocence and cries out against the inequities of Yahweh's wrath. In a sense, the *Book of Job* defines Job as an innocent man, and thus the response of his friends is by definition inadequate. Two other answers emerge: The prolog suggests that Job's suffering is a test of his faith. The epilog suggests that suffering has a redemptive capacity. By accepting his suffering with continued faith, Job is brought into a restored state. Thus, while Job cannot agree with his friends' interpretation of his suffering as punishment for his offenses, the book concludes with a continued support of the religious point of view. God is omnipotent, and, in the face of seeming meaningless suffering, the inscrutable ways must be accepted faithfully rather than doubted. Ultimately, it is that very acceptance that becomes a mechanism of soteriological significance.

We probably all remember reading Thornton Wilder's *The Bridge of San Luis Rey*, which concerns the quest for continued religious meaning in the face of tragedy. A suspension bridge collapses, and the five people who happen to be on the bridge at that particular moment fall to their deaths. Is there meaning to be found in this tragedy? The priest in the story, who conducts a close analysis of each of the victim's lives, is interested to see if there is some pattern of meaning that emerges that might explain why these particular persons lost their lives, why they happened to be the ones on the bridge at that particular moment. The conclusion seems at best ambiguous and is not unlike Wisdom's parable of the garden and the gardener. To the priest, the five victims' lives indicate that each had reached what appeared to be a concluding point, a type of closure. The significance for the priest is that there is then some meaning in these peoples' death. If the collapse of the bridge was truly an accident, and if it was purely by chance that those particular people happened to be on the bridge at that moment, then the priest's religious worldview has no meaning! Perhaps, however, another person looking at the same data would have concluded that there was no closure of the victims' lives. Wilder appears to end his novel in basic agreement with the priest—the distribution of suffering is not random; yet in many ways the question is left open. Could we, for example, compile our own *Bridge of San Luis Rey* document concerning the crash of the Japan Airlines jet in the summer of 1985, or the catastrophic loss of life in the Mexico City earthquake? What of the Holocaust, of the present threat of nuclear confrontation, or nuclear winter? At what point does suffering reach such magnitude that the human response cries out the falsity of the religious worldview? Or, at whatever point, is there still a sense of meaning, an affirmation that we live in a world of moral good and purpose?

How we respond to the seeming capriciousness of tragedy and suffering indicates our ultimate understanding of the soteriological structure of reality, or lack of any such structure. With remarkably few (if any) exceptions, the religious response, in the face of extraordinary adversity, is to cling to the religion's structure of meaning. With tenacious perseverance, the religious worldview deepens its own understanding of the human condition and of the response called for in time of need. As we examine the breadth of religious traditions, we see that suffering is a central problem, which all too universally defines the human condition.

For some, suffering takes on abstract meanings, but it is never a merely theoretical problem; its reality is too overwhelming. The apostle Paul exemplifies the Christian acceptance of the reality of suffering when he says, "I shall therefore prefer to find my joy and pride in the very things that are my weakness and then the power of Christ will come and rest upon me. Hence I am well content, for Christ's sake, with weakness, contempt, persecution, hardship, and frustration; for when I am weak, then I am strong."[5] The Buddha is said to have used the metaphor of the arrow to exhort his disciples to eliminate suffering. When one has been hit by an arrow, is it appropriate to discuss the type of tip of the arrow, or the wood of the shaft? No! The sole concern is to remove the arrow in order to eliminate the person's suffering. Thus it is with the teachings of the Buddha. They are not designed for theoretical or abstract discussion. Their sole purpose is to eliminate suffering. This remains a universal concern in religious responses.

There is a certain dominant interpretation of suffering that, at a very general level, occurs in both Hindu and Buddhist traditions. Typically, Hinduism and Buddhism are held up as representative of Eastern religious thoughts, and certainly to a degree this is true. Yet, if we want a full accounting of an Eastern model, we must also look to Confucianism. In many respects, Confucianism has been the dominant tradition underlying the religious worldview and values of much of East Asia. Hinduism and Buddhism are very important to understand, but they are only part of the Eastern model.

## Suffering in the Hindu Model

The *Bhagavad Gita* is, in many ways, the most universal of Hindu scriptures and represents a synthesis of many points of view within the Hindu tradition. The *Gita* involves a great battle, about to commence between two factions of the same family. Arjuna, one of the warriors and a central figure of the scripture, seeing relatives on the other side, concludes that he cannot fight. He enters into conversation with his charioteer Krishna (who later reveals himself to be the central divinity of the scripture) about his obligation as one born of the warrior class. Krishna instructs Arjuna about his duty and, in the process, explains to Arjuna the nature of man and reality. Part of this teaching, which is based upon the Vedic *Upanishads*, stresses what is known as *jnana-yoga*, or the Way of Knowledge, which teaches that if we can only correct the way we see things, then such things as suffering will have much less impact on us. Krishna's instructions are based in the monastic interpretation of the *Upanishads*, which sees ultimate reality, *Brahman*, and the individual self, *atman*, as identical. The problem of human existence in the world is that we do not see the real self, the true self, and as a result we live with all the mistaken impressions of a false self. We think that what happens to us and to others is actual, that it *is* something happening to our selves. But, Krishna counsels Arjuna, "You grieve for those who should not be mourned. . . . The learned do not grieve for the dead or for the living. Never, indeed, was there a time when I was not, nor when you were not, nor these lords of men. Never, too, will there be a time, hereafter, when we shall not be."[6]

The true self, the *atman*, is eternal. One need not grieve for the loss of life, for it is of little consequence in relation to the true self. Krishna advises Arjuna of his duty as a warrior to fight, but within the framework of this teaching. "Therefore fight, O Bharata. He who regards him as a slayer, as he who regards him as slain— both of them do not know the truth; for this one neither slays nor is slain. He is not born, nor does he die at any time; nor, having once come to be will he again come not to be. He is unborn, eternal, permanent, and primeval; he is not slain when the body is slain."[7]

For the person who lacks this perspective, suffering is real, because human life is seen as an end unto itself. But if insight into or knowledge of the true self, the *atman*, has been gained, then the meaning of whatever might befall one or those around one is always relative to the true self. This model needs also to be placed within the setting of the theory of *karma* and rebirth. As we perpetuate our selves, the conditions of each moment are the product of the previous moment or moments. Thus, as we act, so do we become. In turn, the context and condition of each individual life is determined by the preceding life. Only when we gain insight into the true self, the *atman*, will the duality, and thus the separateness and individuality, of the self be relinquished. In turn, the perpetuation of rebirth will stop.

The attitudes toward suffering and the proper response to it in this setting are: first, that suffering is brought about primarily through a mistaken view of the self and the world. Our common perception of self is dualistic. We therefore attribute a level of reality to the self as we know it that in its true nature it does not have. Suffering affects only the false self; therefore, we are ultimately mistaken when we attribute reality to the nature of suffering. As long as we perpetuate the false sense of self, then we will suffer, or appear to suffer. Of course, to the false self this suffering is real enough, and it is here that some positive good can be seen in suffering. Suffering can produce the thought that what we take as the real self is in fact not the real self, and can thus occasion movement toward insight into the real self. In this sense, suffering can act as a catalyst to precipitate the intention toward spiritual liberation.

It can also be the ground for the motivation of compassion and caring toward those who feel their own suffering or suffer because of seeing suffering in those who are nearest to them. But, the basis of this caring is to bring the person to the perspective where they will realize that the nature of their suffering is grounded in a false sense of the self and its reality.

There is, however, another response. Hinduism is often portrayed as recalcitrant to change and presented historically as offering little in the way of bettering conditions for those who suffer. This interpretation has focused on the *varnasrama-dharma* structure of Classical Hinduism, which states that the caste one is born into is appropriate to one's own *karma* and that whatever inequities exist betweeen the castes—and thus the level of suffering for those who are oppressed—is, in a way, justified. It might be said that those who suffer deserve the station of life they have been born into, and the conditions of that life, which they must endure. From this perspective, it would be incorrect to try to create an egalitarian society. In the very structure of the universe, inequities are inherent; egalitarian goals serve only to obfuscate legitimate distinctions.

This is a controversial area of interpretation and runs the risk of engaging one in a normative enterprise of comparing different religious traditions and passing judgment as to which is better or worse. Let me simply say that if, in a very different tradition, the dominant interpretation of suffering focuses on suffering as punishment for wrongdoing, then there, too, there seems little justification for stepping in and aiding or rectifying suffering; it is an intended act of God. Within Hinduism, the focus of response certainly remains on the individual who is enduring suffering coming to a perspective on the nature of suffering—i.e., its ultimate falseness—and thus adjusting to the experience of suffering by cultivating greater and greater detachment. This path remains central, whether one is of high caste or at the bottom of the spiritual and political scale. Only knowledge of the true self will eventually eliminate the experience of suffering.

## Suffering in the Buddhist Model

The Four Noble Truths, the quintessential teaching of the Buddha, specify suffering as the major defining characteristic of the human condition. The Four Noble Truths function as a kind of medical diagnosis, identifying the problem of the human condition. The first Noble Truth states that the human condition is sorrow and suffering: "And this is the Noble Truth of Sorrow. Birth is sorrow, age is sorrow, disease is sorrow, death is sorrow, contact with the unpleasant is sorrow, separation from the pleasant is sorrow, every wish unfulfilled is sorrow—in short all the five components of individuality are sorrow."[8]

Little is excluded in this first Noble Truth! It thoroughly probes the recesses of one's activities, ferreting out those that, with only some little thought, may be seen within the context of sorrow and suffering; for example, the pleasure we derive from activities or objects that have involved the suffering of others. Or the degree to which pleasure puts us in bondage to the object of our pleasure, or simply the degree to which material things ultimately do not satisfy our innermost feelings.

The second Noble Truth identifies the cause of this sorrow and suffering: "And this is the Noble Truth of the Arising of Sorrow. It arises from craving which leads to rebirth, which brings delight and passion, and seeks pleasure now here, now there—the craving for sensual pleasure, the craving for continued life, the craving for power."[9] Sorrow and suffering arise because of our craving, which is ultimately bound up with a profound ignorance, *avidya*—the religious problematic in the Buddhist tradition. Essentially, we are ignorant of who we really are. We therefore perpetuate a false self that pushes itself on from moment to moment and life to life and will continue to do so until the self has seen the self for what it truly is. Ignorance is best defined in Early Buddhism by the Four Perverted Views: We take as permanent what is actually impermanent; we take as self what is actually not self; we take as attractive what is actually repulsive; and we take as happiness what is actually ill. Such ignorance pushes us on and, in the Buddhist theory of causation or dependent co-origination, is seen as the cause for the arising and perpetuation of self and the world.

The cure to this malady of profound ignorance is to be found in the third Noble Truth: "And this is the Noble Truth of the Stopping of Sorrow. It is the complete stopping of that craving, so that no passion remains, leaving it, being emancipated from it, being realized from it, giving no place to it."[10] This is the Noble Truth of Nirvana—the elimination of ignorance and, therefore, the cessation of karmic activity; and with this, the breaking off of the perpetuation of the self's deluded view of the world and itself. From the Buddhist point of view, breaking the bond of ignorance of self and world is, in turn, breaking the bond of suffering and sorrow.

The fourth Noble Truth is the prescription—how one gets to this point: "And this is the Noble Truth of the Way which leads to the Stopping of Sorrow. It is the Noble Eightfold Path—Right Views, Right Resolve, Right Speech, Right Conduct, Right Livelihood, Right Effort, Right Mindfulness, and Right Concentration."[11] Here we find effort directed toward the way one lives in realms of activity and thought, and the role this will play in reaching the perspective that will bring about enlightenment—knowledge of the true nature of things—and thus remove the cloud of ignorance that shrouds our perception. In this Buddhist framework, the role of suffering is central. It is the primary perception of the human condition; yet it remains also a false view of the nature of things.

A story prominent throughout Buddhism concerns the suffering of a mother, Kisagotami, at the death of her only child. The mother is frantically seeking medicine to restore her child to life.

Someone advises her to visit Gautama, the Buddha, for he is said to have medicine.

> Kisagotami went to Gautama, and doing homage to him, said, "Lord and master, do you know any medicine that will be good for my boy?" Gautama replied, "I know of some." She asked, "What medicine do you require?" He said, "I want a handful of mustard seed." The girl promised to procure it for him, but Gautama continued, "I require some mustard seed taken from a house where no son, husband, parent or slave has died." The girl said, "Very good," and went to ask for some at the different houses, carrying the dead body of her son astride on her hips. The people said, "Here is some mustard seed, take it." Then she asked, "In my friend's house, has there died a son, a husband, a parent or a slave?" They replied, "Lady, what is this that you say! The living are few, but the dead are many!" Then she went to other houses, but one said, "I have lost a son"; another, "I have lost my parents"; another, "I have lost my slave!"[12]

Kisagotami is able to find no home free of suffering; she sees that she is not alone in her grief. She abandons the body of her son and returns to the Buddha, who says to her, "You thought that you alone had lost a son; the law of death is that among all living creatures there is no permanence."[13] In this parable, the cure to the personal experience of suffering is to realize its universal nature and ultimately to see that suffering itself is a creation of our own ignorance. As with the Hindu tradition, the reality of suffering is relative to our own wisdom and insight into the nature of things.

This does not eliminate the experience of suffering for those of us who have yet to gain insight and dispel our own profound ignorance. The Buddhist tradition has been rather attentive to the need to bring compassion and caring to people's ignorance. Certainly, it can be argued in the abstract that suffering is of one's own making and that, ultimately, facing that suffering head on is the only way to penetrate the profound ignorance that hides the truth, but there is also a tenderness in the compassion and caring of the Buddhist to bring an end to suffering. This is particularly represented in the Bodhisattva figure of the later Mahayana Buddhist tradition. The Bodhisattva has vowed that he will not enter Nirvana until all beings have been brought, from their suffering, to the point of Nirvana. This ideal is represented in the vow the Bodhisattva takes, quoted here in part:

All creatures are in pain. . . . All that mass of pain and evil karma I take in my own body. . . . I take upon myself the burden of sorrow. . . . Assuredly I must bear the burdens of all beings . . . for I have resolved to save them all. I must save the whole world from the forest of birth, old age, disease, and rebirth, from misfortune and sin, from the round of birth and death, from the toils of heresy.[14]

In standard Mahayana doctrine, the Bodhisattva has culti-vated the Six *Paramitas* or Perfections; two of these are wisdom and compassion. In the Bodhisattva's vow, we see infinite compas-sion for all beings. Yet, this is combined with his own wisdom, which shows him that ultimately there are no beings whatsoever, and there is in fact no suffering. A paradox? Perhaps, but mainly an example of the levels of truth in Buddhism, and thus the relative levels of experience and knowledge. The fact that the Bodhisattva knows that there are no beings does not assuage the suffering of one who still views himself as a being. Therefore, compassion must be exercised to bring those beings to the point of realizing that their suffering can be thrown off. The Bodhisattva ideal becomes a model for moral action on the part of the Buddhist. The commit-ment is to eliminate suffering and sorrow. The context is one of levels of truth and, ultimately, the relativity of the state of suffering, but there is a keen awareness that for those who suffer, suffering is real enough. The remedy to suffering is to ferret out those ele-ments that produce suffering, but, in the short run, there is a turning toward the Eightfold Path. We gradually educate ourselves as well as others in the nature of our mistaken view of ourselves and the world, with the understanding that gradually, over ex-tended lifetimes, the self will come to understand itself. Concur-rently, suffering will cease on its own, as its lack of substantial reality becomes clearer.

In both the Hindu and Buddhist models, there is emphasis on the ultimate lack of reality of suffering. Suffering is viewed as a relative condition, precipitated primarily by our ignorance of our true natures. Suffering is, in that sense, only a problem when we take ourselves and the world as ends unto themselves. Suffering is then inevitable and inexorable. The antidote, in both traditions, is the correct knowledge of the true nature of things.

Although both Hinduism and Buddhism tend to express this nontheistically, they would be in fundamental agreement with St.

Augustine when he says, in the *Confessions*, "Wherever the soul of man turns, unless towards God, it cleaves to sorrow, even though the things outside itself to which it cleaves may be things of beauty."[15] Suffering is of our own making, and its resolution lies in our own spiritual cultivation. The positive role suffering can play is to precipitate more rapidly our intention to seek release from our ignorance and freedom from our sorrow. As soon as release is attained, suffering is seen to hold no further sway over us. Ultimately, it is a mere phantom of a world of unreality we, through ignorance, take all too seriously.

## Suffering in the Confucian Model

A very different image of the meaning of suffering can be seen in the East Asian Confucian view. Here, the reality of suffering is accepted, just as the reality of the world is accepted. The focus is not to diminish metaphysically the role of suffering but to provide a specific daily response to its reality.

The Confucian vision seeks to restore a moral society. It has traditionally looked to the past, to a period of sage rulers, as the model whereby to guide this restoration. The focus of such efforts has centered around the process of learning and self-cultivation, with the aim of developing and transforming oneself into a moral person and society into a moral society. The moral person, called a *chün-tzu* (noble person) or a *sheng-jen* (sage), becomes the exemplar. Classical formulations of the proper virtues to develop often refer to a set of five human relations—king/subject, father/son, husband/wife, elder brother/younger brother, and friend/friend. These become the focus of learning and self-cultivation, but the seminal issue is to develop the moral nature of the individual, so that he or she will be able to respond with appropriate sensitivity and responsibility to any situation. Thus, Confucius stresses certain key virtues. One is to act with *i*, righteousness, a word that comes very close to our meaning of conscience, a kind of internal guide to what is right and wrong. *I* is held in sharp contrast to *li* (profit) and *yung* (utility), suggesting that one's intent is that which is morally right, rather than profitable, or expedient and utilitarian. One is to act with *li*, ritual propriety, a subtle virtue, stressing that ritual is not just prescribed activity, but rather inward feelings and sensitivities. *I* is a demonstration of propriety—the inner reflection of respect for others. One is also to cultivate the virtue of *jen*, translated as goodness or humaneness. The Chinese written character is composed of the component for person and that for the number two; thus, it literally means person doubled, or "person-to-person–ness," suggesting the inherent moral nature of the relationship of one person to another. *Jen* is the most frequently used characterization of the moral person; it is described as the single thread that runs throughout the teachings. When *jen* is defined by Confucius, he uses two other virtues to describe it—*chung* and *shu*, translated as altruism and reciprocity. A number of teachings are summarized in the moral injunction spoken of by Confucius: "Never do to others what you would not like them to do to you."[16] Herein lie the grounds for compassion and caring.

And what of the response to suffering? Within the religious structure of Confucianism, *T'ien* (Heaven) has given humanity its moral nature. Our understanding of compassion and caring is best seen within the ramifications of the virtues we have discussed, and their relation to the five special moral relations. From the Confucian perspective, *jen*, goodness or humaneness, comes very close to our understanding of compassion and caring—one has a moral (and religious) responsibility toward others and cultivates an ability to empathize with their plight. The only qualification of this is the priority Confucius sets on certain specific moral relations: essentially, relations with those who are closest family. Only afterwards does *jen* extend to the larger framework of humanity as a whole. There are, then, priorities in moral response, and a need to deal first with issues immediately at hand.

Confucius was severely criticized by the philosopher Mo Tzu for this point of view. Mo Tzu advoates *chien-ai* (universal love) and accuses Confucians of cultivating partiality.[17] The Confucian rebuttal is that, while universal love is an admirable goal, unless there is a specific set of relations within which to apply the notion of love, it will not develop in any relation. If one perfects such feeling within a particular moral relation, then it can logically be applied outward to the widest possible circle. The disciple Tzu-lu asks Confucius about the qualities of the noble person; Confucius replies: "He cultivates in himself the capacity to be diligent in his tasks." Tzu-lu said, 'Can he not go further than that?' The Master said: 'He cultivates in himself the capacity to ease the lot of other people.' Tzu-lu said, 'Can he not go further than that?' The Master said, 'He cultivates in himself the capacity to ease the lot of the whole populace.' "[18] In another passage in the *Analects*, there is a clear indication of the degree to which the noble person takes on the burden of the world. "Master Tseng said: 'The true knight of the way must perforce be both broad-shouldered and stout of heart; his burden is heavy and he has far to go. For Goodness is the burden he has taken upon himself and must we not grant that it is a heavy one to bear.' "[19]

We do not find in the classical Confucian tradition, or even in the later neo-Confucian tradition, a sustained explanation of the origins or metaphysics of suffering. We find instead acceptance of suffering as a fact of existence. For Confucius, human obligation to the sufferer is met by the moral responsibility inherent in the noble person's cultivation of moral nature, ultimately the fulfillment of Heaven's Way. The primary focus remains perfecting one's relation to those who are in a special moral relation, but the vision already exists of the moral person's capacity to serve as a model for the populace at large and, indeed, to see his own obligation and responsibility in the largest possible sphere. These same themes are developed in a much fuller fashion by Mencius, the second major teacher of the tradition. In fact, it is Mencius' forms of the discussion and argument that have been accepted as the primary and even orthodox Confucian position.

*Human Nature and Responsibility*

Mencius, unlike Confucius, is far more interested in the actual nature of humanity, specifically what it is that is instilled in that nature by Heaven and how this may be developed. For Mencius, it becomes critical to demonstrate the inherent goodness of human nature. We have first the argument with the philosopher Kao Tzu, who feels that human nature is neutral at birth; goodness is the result of training. For example, Kao Tzu argues that human nature is like water trapped in a whirlpool: If you open a channel for it on the west, it will flow west, on the east and it will flow east. This is because water is neutral: It will flow whatever way the channel provides. Mencius replies by suggesting that the critical issue is that the water flows downward; this is part of the nature of water. By analogy, goodness is inherent in human nature.

> Human nature is good just as water seeks low ground. There is no man who is not good; there is no water that does not flow downwards. Now in the case of water, by splashing it one can make it shoot up higher than one's forehead and by forcing it one can make it stay on a hill. How can that be the nature of water? It is the circumstances being what they are. That man can be made bad shows that his nature is no different from that of water in this respect.[20]

Probably the most famous example of the Mencian theory of the goodness of human nature is his example of the child about to fall into the well. Appropriately, for our purposes, it is an example of human response to a situation of potential suffering and tragedy.

> Suppose a man were, all of a sudden, to see a young child on the verge of falling into a well. He would certainly be moved to compassion, not because he wanted to get in the good graces of the parents, nor because he wished to win the praise of his fellow villagers or friends, nor yet because he disliked the cry of the child. From this it can be seen that whoever is devoid of the heart of compassion is not human, whoever is devoid of the heart of courtesy and modesty is not human, and whoever is devoid of the heart of right and wrong is not human. The heart of compassion is the germ of benevolence; the heart of shame, of dutifulness; the heart of courtesy and modesty, of the observance of ties; the heart of right and wrong, of wisdom. Man has these four germs just as he has four limbs.[21]

These four innate responses, called the Four Beginnings, *ssu-tuan*, are the inherent moral nature bestowed in each of us. They are only germs or seeds, and thus they must be cultivated and developed to full maturity and manifestation. Evil is still possible if they are neglected or ignored, but those who, through learning and self-cultivation, foster these virtues can become as the sages themselves, a goal of immediate moral significance and ultimate religious significance. "For a man to give full realization to his heart is for him to understand his own nature, and a man who knows his own nature will know Heaven. By retaining his heart and nurturing his nature he is serving Heaven."[22]

Another classic passage from Mencius relates directly to the heart's feeling toward suffering, in this case, the suffering of animals. The king is sitting in the upper portion of his hall, when someone leads an ox through the lower part. Seeing this, the king inquires where the ox is going. He learns that the ox is to be sacrificed, so that its blood may be used to consecrate a new bell. The king demands that the ox be spared: "Spare it. I cannot bear to see it shrinking with fear, like an innocent man going to the place of execution." The man leading the ox asks if the consecration of the bell should be cancelled. The king responds that that would be out of the question and suggests that a sheep should be substituted for the ox.[23] The initial question of the passage revolves around the substitution of the sheep for the ox. How is the apparent arbitrariness of this decision to be explained? Is it an effort to economize by using a smaller animal? If the king were truly concerned about the sacrifice of the ox, how could he permit the sacrifice of the sheep? Mencius provides an explanation of the kings bewilderment. "It is the way of the benevolent man. You saw the ox but not the lamb. The attitude of a gentleman towards animals is this: once having seen them alive, he cannot bear to seem them die, and once having heard their cry he cannot bear to eat their flesh."[24]

The discussion returns to the sensitivity shown toward the ox. It is similar to the case of the child about to fall into the well. In both cases, the true nature of humanity reveals itself; the inherent goodness is manifest in the inability to endure the suffering of others. Mencius's actual motive in the story of the king, however, is to suggest that if he has sensitivity toward animals, then how much more should he have toward fellow humans? "Your bounty is sufficient to reach to animals, yet the benefits of your government fail to reach the people."[25] To manifest truly the inner nature of goodness, the king cannot limit his sensitivity to animals but must show his greatest concern for the suffering of his people. "Treat the aged of your family in a manner befitting their venerable age and extend this treatment to the aged of other families; treat your own young in a manner befitting their tender age and extend this to the young of other families."[26] Ultimately, both stories fall back on a basic ethical claim, stated succinctly in a later part of the text. "No man is devoid of a heart sensitive to the suffering of others."[27] This is perhaps the basic ethical claim of the Confucian tradition, and its initial formulation by Mencius is repeated throughout the history of the tradition. It is this heart that cannot bear the suffering of others that, from the Confucian perspective, represents our own deepest nature, which by definition is good and links us ultimately to the moral structure of the universe. In the heart that cannot bear to see the suffering of others lies the capacity for compassion and for caring.

## The Neo-Confucian Quest

I would like to draw to a close with several examples of the later development of the Confucian tradition, known generally as neo-Confucianism. Here, Confucianism has sought consciously to create a larger framework of metaphysical discussion. We are no longer discussing simply the capacity for goodness in human nature and its bestowal by Heaven. Instead, the discussion becomes one of inherent metaphysical structures that see Heaven, *T'ien,* as *T'ien-li,* the principle of Heaven, an abstract metaphysical structure of moral goodness that is the very root and foundation of the universe. Each and every thing, each and every person, shares in the principle of Heaven. The Four Beginnings of goodness are the specific manifestation of the principle of Heaven and are found in either nature or the mind, depending on the particular school of neo-Confucianism. The result of this development is to see more clearly the metaphysical grounds for discussion of the unity of the microcosm—the individual—and the macocosm—the universe.

One of the clearest examples of the neo-Confucian vision of the unity underlying the universe, and a call to moral action, is the work called the *Hsi-ming* (Western Inscription), by the Sung dynasty neo-Confucian author, Chang Tsai. The first few lines of the work establish the vision and the moral responsibility:

> Heaven is my father and Earth is my mother and even such a small creature as I find an intimate place in their midst. Therefore that which fills the universe I regard as my body and that which directs the universe I consider as my own nature. All people are my brothers and sisters and all things are my companions. . . . Respect the aged—this is the way to treat them as elders should be treated. Show affection toward the orphaned and the weak—this is the way to treat them as the young should be treated. . . . Even those who are tired, infirm, crippled, or sick, those who have no brothers or children, wives or husbands all are my brothers who are in distress and have no one to turn to.[28]

From the Confucian perspective, we stand in a close relation, metaphysically, to the universe. That which unites all things ultimately is the very moral nature of the universe. Chang Tsai, as other new-Confucians, fully accepts Mencius' theory of human nature and thereby the moral responsibility to serve our fellow humans. The *Western Inscription* is in many ways an exemplification of the heart that cannot bear to see the suffering of others, and thus of the compassion and caring that are inherent in the Confucian quest.

Ch'eng Hao, another prominent neo-Confucian of the Sung dynasty, puts the same issue a little differently, making the virtue of *jen*, goodness, the central uniting structure of micro- and macrocosm. "The man of *jen* regards Heaven and Earth and all things as one body. To him there is nothing that is not himself. Since he has recognized all things as himself, can there be any limit to his humanity? . . . Therefore to be charitable and to assist all things is the foundation of the sage."[29] Compassion and caring are implicit within the sage's capacity to realize his own nature and thereby his unity with all things.

Finally, Wang Yang-ming, of the Ming dynasty, illustrates a similar sense of responding to those in need. In his commentary to the *Ta-Hsüeh, (Great Learning)*, Yang-ming develops the ramifications of the view of a moral universe and therefore moral human nature.

> The great man regards Heaven and Earth and the myriad things as one body. He regards the world as one family and the country as one person. . . . That the great man can regard Heaven, Earth and the myriad things as one body is not because he deliberately wants to do so, but because it is natural to the humane nature of his mind that he do so. . . . Therefore when he sees a child about to fall into a well he cannot help a feeling of alarm and commiseration. This shows that his humanity forms one body with the child.[30]

Yang-ming sees the special moral relations as the basis for extending compassion and caring to all:

> Therefore, only when I love my father, the father of others and the father of all men can my humanity really form one body with my father, the fathers of others, and the fathers of all men. When it truly forms one body with them, then the clear character of filial piety will

be manifested. Only when I love my brother, the brother of others, and the brothers of all men can my humanity really form one body with my brother, the brothers of others, and the brothers of all men. When it truly forms one body with them, then the clear character of brotherly respect will be manifested. Everything from ruler, minister, husband, wife and friends to mountains, rivers, spiritual beings, birds, animals, and plants should be truly loved in order to realize my humanity that forms one body with them . . . and I will really form one body with Heaven, Earth and the myriad things."[31]

## Conclusion

The Confucian tradition presents a different model of an Eastern understanding of suffering. While both Hinduism and Buddhism regard suffering as central to their religious concerns, they also tend to interpret suffering as of a qualified nature. It is a condition that is created and experienced primarily because humans are ignorant of their own deep spiritual roots. Suffering, as I argued earlier, has only a relative status. Responses to it suggest that in one sense it is something that the individual has received because of past deeds; i.e., suffering is earned. But it can also be the basis for turning to more serious questions of the ultimate spiritual liberation of the self; i.e., it can move the individual toward the soteriological goal and can provide the foundation for compassionate action toward others. These questions seem to play little role in the Confucian response. The Confucian does not attempt to see the world as anything less than real. In turn, there is a level of metaphysical reality assigned to human activity that does not call into question the status of suffering. In this sense, suffering is not relative to the ignorance of the true nature of the self; suffering is simply a characteristic of human existence. The Confucian quest is to respond to this characteristic, and, thus, compassion and caring dominate the Confucian vision.

  In the final analysis, then, we can say that compassion and caring play key roles in the response of the three traditions we have surveyed. If we can go back to the first issue raised, we can see compassion and caring as logical outgrowths of the very nature of the structure of a religious system. We have seen that a religious worldview is remarkably tenacious in its encounter with suffering, even suffering in geometric magnitude. Rather than renounce the religious claim, there is an attempt to give meaning and understanding to the occurrence of suffering. Whether suffering is viewed as real or unreal, ultimately both views are responses that try to provide meaning and, in turn, are part of the responses of the religious worldview. This issuing forth in response is the capacity of the religious tradition to hold compassion and caring as central and salient.

## NOTES

1. Peter Matthiessen, *The Snow Leopard* (New York: Bantam Books, 1978), 22.
2. W. T. Stace, "Man Against Darkness," *Atlantic Monthly* (September 1948): 54–58, quoted in *Ways of Being Religious: Readings for a New Approach to Religion*, eds. F. Streng, C. Lloyd Jr., and J. Allen (Englewood Cliffs, NJ: Prentice-Hall, 1973), 339.
3. Clifford Geertz, "Religion as a Cultural System." In *Reader in Comparative Religion: An Anthropological Approach*, eds. W. Lessa and E. Vogt, 4th ed. (New York: Harper and Row, 1979), 85. See my discussion of Stace and Geertz in R. L. Taylor, *The Confucian Way of Contemplation* (Columbia, South Carolina: University of South Carolina Press, 1988), 64-65.
4. Quoted in John Hick, *Philosophy of Religion* (Englewood Cliffs, NJ: Prentice-Hall, 1963), 97.
5. 2 Corinthians 12:8–10.
6. W. T. deBary, ed., *Sources of Indian Tradition*, vol. 1 (New York: Columbia University Press, 1958), 279.
7. Ibid.
8. Ibid., 99. David Little also cites the Four Noble Truths but with a different translation (p. 54).
9. Ibid.
10. Ibid.
11. Ibid.
12. Quoted in L. Stryk, *The World of the Buddha* (Garden City, NY: Doubleday and Company, 1968), 173.
13. Ibid., 174
14. deBary, *Indian Tradition*, 161. Also cited by Little, but with a different translation (p.69).
15. *The Confessions of St. Augustine* 4:9, quoted in John Bowker, *Problems of Suffering in the Religions of the World* (London: Cambridge University Press, 1970), 90.
16. *Analects* 15:23. See *The Analects of Confucius*, tr. Arthur Waley (New York: Vintage Books, 1938), 198.
17. See Burton Watson, tr., *Mo Tzu: Basic Writings* (New York: Columbia University Press, 1963), 39–49.
18. *Analects* 14:45, Waley, 191.

19. *Analects* 8:7, Waley, 134.
20. *Mencius*,6A:2. See *Mencius* tr. D. C. Lau (Middlesex, Eng.: Penguin Books, 1970), 160.
21. *Mencius* 2A:6. Lau, 82–83.
22. *Mencius* 7A:1. Lau, 182.
23. *Mencius* 1A:7. Lau, 55.
24. Ibid.
25. *Mencius* 1A:7. Lau, 56.
26. Ibid.
27. *Mencius* 2A:6. Lau, 82.
28. W. T. Chan, tr., *Reflections on Things at Hand: The Neo-Confucian Anthology Compiled by Chu Hsi and Lü Tsu-ch'ien* (New York: Columbia University Press, 1967), 76–77.
29. W. T. Chan, *A Source Book in Chinese Philosophy* (Princeton: Princeton University Press, 1963), 530.
30. W. T. Chan, tr., *Instructions for Practical Living and Other Neo-Confucian Writings by Wang Yang-ming* (New York: Columbia University Press, 1963), 272.
31. Chan, *Instructions*, 273.

WILLIAM J. PRIOR

# Compassion: A Critique of Moral Rationalism

## Moral Theory

> A man was going down from Jerusalem to Jericho, and he fell among robbers, who stripped him and beat him, and departed, leaving him half dead. Now by chance a priest was going down that road; and when he saw him he passed by on the other side. So likewise a Levite, when he came to the place and saw him, passed by on the other side. But a Samaritan, as he journeyed, came to where he was, and when he saw him, he had compassion, and went to him and bound up his wounds, pouring on oil and wine; and then he set him on his own beast and brought him to an inn, and took care of him. And the next day he took out two denarii and gave them to the innkeeper, saying, "Take care of him; and whatever more you spend, I will repay you when I come back."[1]

This familiar parable captures precisely and with brilliant simplicity an essential aspect of morality. It is not exclusively or even primarily a religious story: The representatives of organized religion are not cast in a favorable light; the hero is a member of a nation of religious outcasts; and he does not justify his actions by appeal to religious principles. The story does illustrate the religious commandment that we love our neighbor as ourselves; but secular moralists as well as religious thinkers can endorse this principle. When I say, then, that the story captures an essential aspect of morality, I am not referring only to Christian morality. Rather, the story appeals to moral intuitions shared by civilized people of many

33

religious and cultural backgrounds, including those who profess no religious faith at all.

In the story, one man, through no fault of his own, finds himself in dire need; another man, a stranger and under no special obligation to him, provides the required assistance, and saves his life. The actions of the Samaritan are clearly and unambiguously good. Their goodness is not dependent on the cultural values or customs of the ethnic group to which he belongs; we need know nothing of these to recognize that he does the right thing.

The Samaritan displays a virtuous character in his actions. He is benevolent, generous, and (though the story does not emphasize this point) possesses practical wisdom: He is able to find and follow a course of action that benefits the robbers' victim. He does not display qualities of heroism beyond the reach of most people; these are not required. He only does "what any decent man would do" in the situation. For this reason, he is a realistic model for us: We can see ourselves in him (though perhaps ourselves as we would like to be rather than as we are).

The Samaritan is an admirable character, simply because he does what is right. But why does he act this way? Why does not he, like the Levite and the priest, "pass by on the other side"? Surely, the plight of the victim is as aesthetically unpleasant to him as it must have been to them; surely, his business was as pressing as theirs, and the costs of going out of his way to help as great. There are no witnesses to shame him into right action; none, that is, except the victim, and he is already "half-dead." Why does the Samaritan succeed in moral conduct where others fail?

The story tells us that when the Samaritan saw the victim, he had compassion for him. It is that compassion that engages his virtues of benevolence, generosity, and practical wisdom, and that causes him to act rightly. The Samaritan, as we say, was "moved" by compassion; this way of speaking is not mere metaphor. Compassion, like the appetites and other emotions, can be a motive force, a cause of action; though not, of course, a purely physical one. The Levite and the priest, by contrast, seem to lack this sentiment; they see the plight of the victim but are unmoved by it. Therefore, they fail to respond correctly.

The Greek work translated as "compassion" deserves some comment. It is *esplangchnisthē*, from *splangchnizomai*. Literally, it means "to feel in one's innards"—the *splangchna* are the vital organs. To experience compassion is thus to be "touched where one lives." Although "compassion" and "sympathy" carry the root meaning of "suffering with" another, they have come to lack in common usage the connotation of a visceral reaction so prominent in the Greek word. This is unfortunate; for the compassion that motivates us to moral action is, in paradigm, a strong emotion or sentiment with physical components. In our metaphorical classification of psychological qualities, it belongs to the heart rather than to the mind.[2]

Compassion has a place, along with the physical appetites, guilt and pride, greed, and the several varieties of love, among the emotional "springs of action" that cause us to do what we do and live the way we live. It is a sentiment; an emotion, I would suggest, of central importance to morality. If the teaching of the parable is correct and can be generalized, compassion is the emotion that causes us to act well toward others in need. It is brought into play by the presence of suffering and leads us to act to alleviate that suffering.[3]

It is not sufficient to produce right action in itself; good intentions are not enough. They must be coupled with the virtues if we are to act well. Had the Samaritan been compassionate but a miser, he would not have paid for the victim's room at the inn, and the victim would not have benefited from his compassion. Had the Samaritan been unable to figure out the proper course of action to aid the victim, he might have done him more harm than good. He needed both generosity and practical wisdom, as well as compassion, to act well.[4]

Nor is compassion always necessary to produce right action. Kant describes the hypothetical case of an unhappy philanthropist:

> Suppose then the mind of this friend of mankind to be clouded over with his own sorrow so that all sympathy with the lot of others is extinguished, and suppose him still to have the power to benefit others in distress, even though he is not touched by their trouble because he is sufficiently absorbed with his own; and now suppose that, even though no inclination moves him any longer, he nevertheless tears himself from this deadly insensibility and performs the action without any inclination at all, but solely from duty—then for the first time his action has genuine moral worth.[5]

Kant is surely wrong to insist that only actions motivated by duty have moral worth; he is surely right, however, to claim that there are cases of moral conduct of the sort he describes. Indeed, to consider only one case, it is clear that we often make charitable contributions without being caused to do so by a sentiment of compassion for those who will be aided by our gift. People of a generous temperament, in fact, make such donations habitually; fortunately for the world's charitable organizations and those they aid.

Nonetheless, I would urge, such cases are parasitic on cases of the sort described in the parable. We would not know that the action of Kant's philanthropist was good without the guidance of our sentiment of compassion. It is because we feel, and recognize the appropriateness of, compassion in cases such as that of the Samaritan that we are able to judge the morality of actions in which the sentiment does not occur.

As the parable indicates, compassion is not a universal phenomenon. The Levite and the priest do not have it; the Samaritan does.⁶ It is nonetheless a natural human sentiment. We have no difficulty in recognizing the Samaritan's response as the natural one, and the response of the Levite and priest as unnatural, deficient; and this would be so even if a large number of people responded "unnaturally."

In describing compassion as a natural sentiment, I am using the word "natural" in a normative, evaluative sense. Compassion is natural in that it is part of the emotional constitution of a well-developed, psychologically healthy person. Lack of compassion constitutes a deviation from this norm; people without compassion are thought to be "missing something" in their emotional makeup. In the same sense, it is natural for a human being to have thirty-two teeth: that is the number a well-developed, physically healthy person has, and the fact that many people have fewer teeth, for whatever reason, does not affect this point. The fact that compassion is natural to humans is important; if, as I suspect, it is part of our biological nature, which becomes manifest in the normal course of human development, ignoring compassion in moral psychology will produce an incorrect picture of the sources of moral activity.

The paradigm of compassion is the response of one human being for another, and the presence of a human form in a condition of suffering is the strongest stimulus to compassion. This is the reason, I think, why films and still photographs of aborted fetuses have such a powerful impact on us, and why this impact is but little affected by claims that fetuses, at least in the early stages of development, do not feel pain. Compassion, being an emotional response, is elicited by sense perception more readily than by reason. Rational argument has at most a limited impact on its occurrence.

Reason cannot "argue us out of" our compassion for human suffering; it can, however, harden us to that suffering by preventing us from acting as our emotions dictate. The Levite and the priest, one imagines, justified their inaction with rational arguments about the comparative urgency of their tasks and the diminished capacity of the "half-dead" victim to suffer. In time, this pattern of "rational" action could lead to the suppression not only of compassion but of the guilt that results from that suppression; but the psychological consequences of such suppression would doubtless be undesirable.[7]

What I have described are facts of moral psychology of which nearly everyone is aware. That we respond morally to cases of suffering and need because we are motivated by a strong sentiment of compassion; that this sentiment is part of our human nature; that it is strongest in cases involving other humans—none of this seems very controversial. Yet, one must look long and hard in the writings of moral philosophers to find an adequate account of compassion and its function. Philosophers, with a provinciality that is perhaps understandable if one considers the nature of our discipline, have focused almost without exception on the role of reason in moral action and justification, and have argued that the goodness or rightness in moral action stems from its rationality. Almost all moral philosophers have been, to some degree, moral rationalists.

Moral rationalism, as I shall call it, is the view that moral goodness and rightness are the products of rationality. The moral rationalist may regard reason as valuable instrumentally, in helping one discover the best course of action; but he also thinks of reason as something intrinsically valuable, as being worthy of respect for its own sake, and as the property that makes human life valuable. The moral rationalist, in other words, sees human life as valuable because human beings possess reason.

There are several varieties of moral rationalism, which differ in their treatment of the emotions. For the Stoics, the highest good was a life guided solely by reason, with the appetites and emotions entirely suppressed. This goal, which was to be achieved only by the stoic sage, was labeled *apatheia*, from which our word "apathy" is derived. The sage was to be "apathetic" in the sense that he was free from the "sufferings" *(pathē)* produced by the emotions; he was to remain unperturbed in all circumstances.

Kant, who was much influenced by the Stoics, also identified goodness with rationality. Kant's moral philosophy is based on several sharp contrasts, one of which is that between reason and inclination. Inclination includes all the motives of selfishness and partiality that lead one to act immorally; but it also includes the sentiment of sympathy and the desire for self-preservation, which lead people to act in accordance with the moral law. Even these positive inclinations, thinks Kant, are devoid of moral worth; for an action to be of moral worth, it must be motivated solely by a sense of duty, and duty is determined by reason rather than inclination. When, as Kant thinks is usually the case, reason and inclination conflict, it is the task of reason to ignore inclination and to issue a moral command that the rational agent must follow: thus, "an action done from duty must altogether exclude the influence of inclination and therewith every object of the will. Hence there is nothing left which can determine the will except . . . the law. . . . I should follow such a law even if all my inclinations are thereby thwarted.[8]

Such theories as these, which bifurcate the human personality so completely, and then ignore the claims of one part altogether, are bound to produce distorted results. The ideal of the completely rational agent is not merely difficult to attain, as both Kant and the Stoics recognized; it is deficient as an ideal. The ideal of the sage led Epictetus, one of the most humane of the Stoic philosophers, to recommend a response to the death of a loved one that is chilling in its inhumanity.

> When anything, from the meanest thing upwards, is attractive or serviceable or an object of affection, remember always to say to yourself, "what is its nature?" If you are fond of a jug, say you are fond of a

jug; then you will not be disturbed if it be broken. If you kiss your child or your wife, say to yourself that you are kissing a human being, for then if death strikes it you will not be disturbed.[9]

Kant's theory led him to prefer the actions of the unhappy philanthropist mentioned above to those of a more sympathetic sort, so that he says

> there are many persons who are so sympathetically constituted that, without any further motive of vanity or self-interest, they find an inner pleasure in spreading joy around them and can rejoice in the satisfaction of others as their own work. But I maintain that in such a case an action of this kind, however dutiful and amiable it may be, has nevertheless no moral worth.[10]

The paradoxical quality of this conclusion, and of Kant's preference for the person who is charitable from duty over the person who is charitable because of a sympathetic constitution, should lead one to conclude that something has gone wrong in his theory. For the harmony between reason and inclination in the case of the cheerful giver, the absence of psychological conflict in his deliberations, and the quality of his inner life all indicate that he, and not the unhappy philanthropist, is the person we would prefer to be or to be around.

Not all moral rationalists are as extreme as the Stoics and Kant. Plato and Aristotle, while giving pride of place to reason in the moral conduct of life, recognize the legitimate place of the emotions and appetites in determining right conduct. Plato, in particular, is exceptional in recognizing psychological harmony among the appetites, emotions, and reason as a moral goal of major importance. Yet, one will vainly search the works of these philosophers for a recognition of compassion as a sentiment that leads to moral action. This fact, I think, accounts for much of the perceived "elitism" of their works. Only in the moral philosophy of David Hume does one find this fact acknowledged; only in Hume's theory are what he calls the principles of sympathy and humanity given their rightful place at the foundation of morality. He writes,

> though reason, when fully assisted and improved, be sufficient to instruct us in the pernicious or useful tendency of qualities and actions,

it is not alone sufficient to produce any moral blame or approbation. Utility is only a tendency to a certain end; and were the end totally indifferent to us, we should feel the same indifference toward the means. It is requisite a *sentiment* should here display itself in order to give a preference to the useful among the pernicious tendencies. This sentiment can be no other than a feeling for the happiness of mankind, and a resentment of their misery, since these are the different ends which virtue and vice have a tendency to promote. Here, therefore, *reason* instructs us in the several tendencies of actions, and *humanity* makes a distinction in favor of those which are useful and beneficial.[11]

Hume was surprised to note that "a theory so simple and obvious could so long have escaped the most elaborate examination" given by moral philosophers to the question of the basis of morality.[12] It is even more surprising that Hume's account of the role of sentiment in morality has received relatively little attention from later moralists. Perhaps Kant's rationalist account of morality was so alluring to later ethicists that they paid scant attention to Hume; perhaps Hume's insights were obscured by the tendency of later students of ethics to treat him, most improperly, as a moral skeptic. Whatever the explanation, Hume's salutary treatment of the role of sentiment in moral judgment has certainly not won the day; modern discussions of ethics are as laden with the assumptions of moral rationalism as were those of earlier times.

## Applying Moral Theory to the Mentally Handicapped

I wish now to exhibit the consequences of moral rationalism for the treatment of certain handicapped populations; for I believe that it is in the treatment of these populations that the defects of moral rationalism and the strengths of the compassionate approach are most clearly seen. I focus on the work of Peter Singer, for Singer is an adherent of moral rationalism, who deals with the treatment of the very handicapped people I wish to discuss. His work shows, particularly clearly, I believe, the limitations of a purely rationalistic approach to ethics.

It may seem strange to classify Singer as a moral rationalist for his general approach to ethics is utilitarian. Utilitarians, while emphasizing the instrumental value of reason in ethics, are not rationalists in my sense of the term; they do not find the source of moral value in reason but in pleasure or (in Singer's case) in the satisfaction of preferences. When Singer discusses the morality of killing, however, he allows that there may be special, nonutilitarian considerations that make killing persons a more serious matter than killing other creatures. Persons, i.e., "rational and self-conscious beings," view themselves as distinct entities with pasts and futures.[13] They have desires about those futures, which merely sentient creatures lack. To kill persons is to frustrate those desires; and if Michael Tooley is right in thinking that to frustrate a person's desire to continue living is to violate that person's right to continued life, to kill a person is to violate his or her right to life. Moreover, only persons are capable of autonomy, which Singer describes as "the capacity to choose, to make and act on one's own decisions. . . . Hence killing a person who does not wish to die fails to respect that person's autonomy."[14]

Although Singer, as we would expect a preference utilitarian to do, connects the right to life and autonomy with desires or preferences, they are the preferences of a certain kind of being—a rational, self-conscious, autonomous person. Although he does not positively endorse the view that persons have special rights that make killing them a more serious matter than killing nonpersons, he says that this view cannot be rejected out of hand and that it must be borne in mind when considering the issue. Whatever Singer may believe in his heart of hearts, he states the case for the special value of personhood persuasively; and, since he ties personhood so closely to rationality, it seems fair to treat him as a moral rationalist.

It is a consequence of Singer's view that only the lives of persons can be regarded as especially valuable or as under the protection of a stringent right to life. Singer is well aware of this consequence; indeed he exploits it in his treatment of several related life and death issues. While he uses what I shall call "the principle of personhood" to argue against killing those nonhuman animals that are persons (a group he believes includes apes, whales, and dolphins, and may also include monkeys, dogs, cats, pigs, seals, and bears)[15], he would allow abortion and infanticide on the grounds that fetuses and infants are not persons.

A newborn baby cannot see itself as a being which might or might not have a future, and so cannot have a desire to continue living. For the same reason, if a right to life must be based on the capacity to want to go on living, a newborn baby cannot have a right to life. Finally, a newborn baby is not an autonomous being, capable of making choices, and so to kill it cannot violate the principle of respect for autonomy. In all this the newborn baby is on the same footing as the fetus, and hence fewer reasons exist against killing both babies and fetuses than exist against killing those who are capable of seeing themselves as distinct entities, existing over time.[16]

In order to justify this conclusion, Singer must and does reject the claims of the fetus and newborn to special rights on grounds of their *potential* personhood. Yet, while it may be possible to take issue with Singer on this score, applying the principle of personhood to human beings who are not persons is unencumbered by such sublety. The moderately to severely mentally retarded, including many with Down's syndrome or spina bifida, will never meet Singer's criteria for personhood, even as adults. Consequently, in Singer's view, the special considerations that argue against killing other humans do not apply to them. The mentally handicapped have no right to life, because they cannot live a rational, autonomous existence.

It is not surprising, therefore, that Singer favors nonvoluntary euthanasia for infants born with these conditions. Singer cites the case of a Down's syndrome infant born with an intestinal blockage. The mother refused to allow surgery to remove the blockage, because she "thought that the retarded infant would be impossible for her to care for and would have a destructive effect on her already shaky marriage."[17] In this case, a child welfare agency obtained a court order requiring the operation. The operation was performed, the baby lived (though in poor health), and was eventually returned to the mother "who felt . . . that she had been done a severe injustice."[18]

Singer does not explicitly claim that this baby should have been put to death; but he clearly regards the efforts to save it as excessive and prompted by a view he regards as without foundation: the doctrine of the sanctity of *human* life (as opposed to the lives of persons). His response to the case is one of anger mixed with disbelief. "In this case a human being was kept alive, against the wishes of her mother, and at a cost of thousands, despite the fact that she would never be able to live an independent life, or to think and talk as normal humans do."[19] He does not say whether the mother's wishes, the expense, or the child's limitations would have been, alone, sufficient to justify the child's death, but he clearly regards them as jointly sufficient. Preserving a child's life under such circumstances, he seems to be telling us, is *prima facie* absurd.[20]

Singer's discussion of the Down's syndrome infant occurs in a chapter on the value of various kinds of life; the discussion of children with spina bifida is part of Singer's treatment of nonvoluntary euthanasia. Therefore, there can be no doubt what his proposed remedy for *this* condition is. Since an infant, whether normal or handicapped, is not a person and therefore has no right to life, the case of keeping it alive depends on other factors, such as the wishes of the parents. But, what if the parents do not want the child to live because it has a debilitating handicap such as spina bifida; and what if there are no other couples willing to adopt the child?

Singer's answer is that if, in the opinion of medical specialists, the life of such a child would be so miserable that it would be wrong to use surgery to keep the child alive (which implies, he says, that the life of such a child is "not worth living"), then "utilitarian principles suggest that it is right to kill such children."[21] According to one version of utilitarianism (the "total" view), even children with less severe defects, such as hemophilia, should be killed if the parents would then go on to have another, normal child, which they would not have if the child with hemophilia continued to live.

Infanticide under such conditions is not much different, Singer argues, from abortion in cases where amniocentesis has revealed a birth defect. "I cannot see how one could defend the view that fetuses may be 'replaced' before birth," he remarks, "but newborn infants may not be."[22] Nor, in his view, is the active killing of such infants much different from the practice of British physician John Lorber, which hastens the death of infants with severe cases of spina bifida by the passive method of withholding medical treatment from them, even to the extent of not administering antibiotics for infections.[23] Singer's treatment of the subject concludes that "the main point is clear: killing a defective infant is not morally equivalent to killing a person. Very often it is not wrong at all."[24]

Singer's views on this subject may already seem shocking enough to ordinary people to occasion their wholesale rejection. He admits as much himself, and states the reason: "The conclusions we have reached in this chapter will shock a large number of readers, for they violate one of the most fundamental tenets of Western ethics—the wrongness of killing innocent human beings."[25] Unfortunately, however, the full consequences of his position have not yet been stated. For, though his discussions in *Practical Ethics* focus on killing handicapped infants, exactly the same considerations apply to killing older children or adults with these conditions. Since they are not persons, there is no reason, in Singer's view, to prolong their lives when the wishes of their guardians, expense, or the prospect of an unhappy future suggest otherwise.

Indeed, Singer's restriction of the right to life to persons requires him to countenance the following horrific scenario proosed by Richard Werner:

> Let us imagine a society that accepts that full moral rights and amenability to moral consideration applies only to persons. . . . Such a society could legitimately declare a national open hunting season on infant orphans and other unwanted nonpersons such as the grossly retarded or insane. They could develop a new gourmet delight "roast unwanted infant." They could begin to establish farms such as one that buys live abortuses, raises them for food, experimentation, or sport. They could take such young children raised from live abortuses, perform brain operations on them so as to be sure that they will never develop (into persons) and then use them as pets, servants, slaves, lab animals, and so on. Indeed, it seems that we could not rule out the wanton killing of or medical experimentation upon infants, severely retarded humans, the extremely mentally ill, certain possible future generations and all other nonperson humans.[26]

Singer's view is not merely shocking; all morally sensitive people will find it abhorrent, even when they have recovered from the initial shock. It is tempting, in light of this universal reaction, to say of Singer's view what Hume said of scholastic metaphysics: "Commit it, then, to the flames; For it can contain nothing but sophistry and illusion."[27]

Yet, Singer is not so easily dealt with. His position, though a minority one, has support within the ranks of philosophers. A philosophical critic, therefore, owes it more than offhand dismissal.

If it is wrong, one wants to know precisely where does it go wrong, and precisely what is wrong with it? It is fair to say, I think, that Singer's would-be critics have been less than completely successful in finding his theory's "fatal flaw."

It is tempting to attack Singer from within the confines of moral rationalism. For it is an extreme view even here, and those committed to the view but not to Singer's conclusions have an interest in showing that their favored theory does not have such repulsive consequences. Thus, one might defend the act-omission distinction against Singer, arguing that the "humane" practice of nontreatment for handicapped individuals does not entail active euthanasia. Alternatively, one might defend a version of the potentiality principle, thereby (if successful) rescuing at least normal fetuses and infants from the consequences of Singer's position. Third, one might argue that parents and others have basic obligations to care for their children, regardless of handicaps.[28]

Finally, one might loosen somewhat the criteria for personhood, so as to admit at least the majority of handicapped humans into the ranks of persons, or argue that the majority of Down's syndrome humans do in fact meet Singer's proposed criteria. There may be other strategies a moral rationalist could employ. Even if they prove successful, however, it is hard to see how every individual now excluded by Singer could be included among the bearers of a right to life.

These approaches, however well-motivated, seem to me to miss the central fault with Singer's view. From the standpoint of the theory I outlined at the beginning of this chapter, it is clear that Singer's view is unacceptable because it is deficient in compassion. By focusing on the direct harm done to the victims of his proposal and by assessing this question in terms of the value of their lives, Singer omits to consider two important factors in the moral evaluation of our treatment of the handicapped: their needs and the effects of such treatment on us.

Singer's justification of active euthanasia for handicapped nonpersons relies on a concept of intrinsic value. Although he would trace the value of autonomy and rationality back to the satisfaction of certain desires, he assumes that there is something intrinsically, objectively good about an individual who possesses these traits and desires. The assumption that rationality and autonomy are intrinsically good is, of course, the root of moral rationalism; I must say, however, that I find it a very dark saying and quite difficult to defend when questioned. When Hume said, "The life of a man is of no greater importance to the universe than that of an oyster," he was attempting to cast doubt on the intrinsic value of rationality.[29] I do not see what answer can be given to Hume, outside a religious context, that does not beg the question. That we value our lives, I have no doubt; that we base our evaluation on the objective occurrence of intrinsically valuable traits seems quite dubious to me.

Yet it is not necessary, from the point of view of compassion, to place some intrinsic value on the lives of handicapped. Compassion is based not on value, but on need. It is not difficult to determine that children having Down's syndrome and spina bifida have needs, even if they lack the conceptual apparatus to articulate them. Among these needs are those of the victim in the Samaritan story: nutrition, shelter, medical care, and the active concern of others. Compassion requires that we respond positively to those needs; and I would hope that I do not have to argue for the claim that killing the needy person does not normally constitute a positive response.

Singer's focus on the direct harm to the patient in these situations causes him to ignore or dismiss questions about the character of the agent; yet these are as central to the compassionate approach as are the patient's needs. The Samaritan, we recall, was a good person; the Levite and the priest were not; and the goodness of the Samaritan's actions depended on the compassion that motivated him as much as on the beneficial results he obtained. Whether or not such compassion is intrinsically and objectively good, from the point of view of the universe, the fact is that we value it, and value persons who have it, while we disvalue those who lack it.

The major problem with Singer's proposal, I would argue, is its necessarily negative effect on us as moral agents. Jonathan Glover, writing on abortion in the *New York Review of Books*, states:

> The most powerful objection to using anesthetized fetuses for research is what this would do to *us*, as researchers or as members of a society where such research went on. We remember the experiments the Nazi doctors were prepared to do on human beings, and wonder about the

strength of the barriers that prevent us from performing atrocities. These barriers must be at least as much emotional as intellectual. We respond to people, whether babies, children, or adults, in ways that make it unthinkable, for most of us, to treat them in the fashion of Nazi doctors. Fetuses, as they develop, start to seem more like babies. Can we be sure that fetal research could be kept in a separate emotional compartment? Or do we risk an erosion of the responses that prevent some of the worst horrors that human beings have shown themselves capable of?[30]

Substitute "handicapped humans" or "fetuses" and "euthanasia" for "medical research" in the above argument and you have a powerful objection to Singer's view. Singer believes that the Nazi specter is just that: a spirit to be exorcized; yet what he says about it is hardly encouraging:

The Nazis committed horrendous crimes; but this does not mean that *everything* the Nazis did was horrendous. We cannot condemn euthanasia just because the Nazis did it, any more than we can condemn the building of new roads for this reason. . . . In the case of Nazism, it was the racist attitude toward "non-Aryans"—the attitude that they were sub-human and a danger to the purity of the Volk—that made the holocaust possible. . . . There is no analogy between this and the proposals of those seeking to legalize euthanasia today.[31]

The first part of the response is an *ignoratio elenchi*: No one argues that everything the Nazis did was horrendous; rather, the argument is that euthanasia was *one* of the horrendous things the Nazis did, and that acceptance of this horror led to acceptance of others, as Glover suggests. Singer's failure to see this argument is of a piece with his failure to see the analogy between regarding some human beings as subhuman on racial grounds and regarding them as subhuman because they do not meet his criteria for personhood.

Yet, Singer is no Nazi, and my objection to the euthanasia of the handicapped is not based on a "slippery slope" argument that such practices will later lead to "serious" moral wrongs. My point is that such treatment of the handicapped, whether active or passive, is itself a serious wrong because it denies the compassionate sentiments within us. To escape the appellation of Nazi is hardly to vindicate one's morality. There are other ways to go wrong; it is bad enough to be grouped with the Levite and priest.

Here, I think, there is an application of the compassionate approach that is particularly relevant to the medical community. We want medical practitioners to have a large measure of patients' trust, for the simple reason that patients will be unwilling to bring their serious medical problems to doctors if they think that they may be killed rather than cured. The business of medicine is to cure illness, where possible; but this business requires a background attitude of care on the part of its practitioners. Medicine has in the past been accorded this requisite trust because its practitioners have shown themselves to be concerned and dedicated. People in medicine today are concerned that this trust may be eroding; I would hesitate to think what might happen to it if hospitals became known as places wherein various sorts of undesirable humans were done away with rather than treated compassionately.

## Conclusion

I have contrasted two approaches to morality, the compassionate approach and that of moral rationalism, both in the abstract and in application to the question of the treatment of certain handicapped people. I have raised objections to the rationalist approach, as presented by Singer, but I am aware that I have said nothing that would likely convince a Singerian of the superiority of the compassionate approach. This is because the two approaches are incommensurable; they value different things and therefore approach ethical choices in different ways. It is thus difficult for any direct argument to take place between proponents of the two views. Indeed, I feel I hardly know what to say to someone who believes that "infants appeal to us because they are small and helpless," and argues that we should "put aside these emotionally moving but strictly irrelevant aspects of the killing of a baby."[32]

If a refutation of a position is the presentation of an argument that the proponent of the position must recognize as fatal to it, I am aware that I have not refuted moral rationalism. I would like to think, however, that I have effectively contrasted it with the compassionate approach and indicated at least some of the advantages of that approach.

I would also like to think that I have sketched two possible directions in which our care of the handicapped might go in the future. You will have no doubt at this point which I prefer; yet it is clear that the choice is not in my hands, but in those of the members of the health sciences. I believe that nothing can conduce to wisdom in this choice so well as a careful delineation of the alternatives themselves; believing, therefore, that I have made at least a step in that direction, I am happy to leave the decision to them.

NOTES

1.  Luke 10:29–35.
2.  This is not to say that compassion is a noncognitive, purely affective element in our psychological makeup. On the contrary, compassion has in it a cognitive component, for it is a response to people in certain situations, and this requires the discrimination of those situations from others. We do not, I think, first recognize the occurrence of these situations by using our cognitive faculties, and then respond to them through our emotions; rather, we recognize and respond by virtue of a single faculty with both cognitive and emotional aspects.
3.  Television recently provided us with an excellent example of how compassion works. The first pictures of the death and suffering caused by the African famine produced a powerful wave of sympathy that led to an outpouring of charitable contributions. Many people, like the Levite and the priest of the parable, tried to deal with the news by turning to another channel; others, like the Samaritan, were moved to aid the victims. The size and strength of the compassionate response, which surprised everyone, was due to the fact that television was able to bring starving people into our living rooms, to make their suffering immediate in a way no other news source can. This is not to say that only the actual presence of suffering or its pictorial representation can elicit a compassionate response; in many cases, the printed word has been sufficient. It is to suggest, however, that the strength of response is proportional to the immediacy of suffering, and also to its being made individual. I am sure that the millions of Americans who sent money to the Red Cross and other famine-relief agencies were not thinking of helping the agencies, but rather the victims displayed on their screens. As we all know, and as the news of the 1985 earthquake in Mexico City confirmed, the casualty figures from a war or natural disaster less effectively engage our sympathy than does the portrayal of a single instance of the suffering they cause.
4.  It should be clear from this statement that I do not regard compassion as replacing reason in the production of right action. I claim only that practical reason and compassion must work together in moral deliberation, and that reason without compassion is likely to lead to morally unacceptable results. Paraphrasing Aristotle, I think that compassion determines the correct end

of our actions in certain situations, and practical reason enables us to determine what is conducive to achieving that end.

5. Immanuel Kant, *Grounding for the Metaphysics of Morals*, tr. James W. Ellington. In *Ethical Philosophy* (Indianapolis: Hackett Publishing, 1983), 11.

6. It is, however, universalizable: we could certainly will that everyone in the parable feel what the Samaritan does. We cannot, on the other hand, will that everyone respond the way the Levite and the priest respond. Those who accept universalizability as a criterion of moral goodness should thus find the Samaritan's response the correct one.

7. So far I have spoken only of cases of compassion involving human beings; but I do not think our sentiment of compassion is limited to them. We can certainly feel compassion for animals; and we are able to respond compassionately to at least some of the alien beings of science fiction. Our compassion for nonhumans is, however, parasitic on our compassion for our own species. We are able to respond sympathetically to an animal caught in a trap because we think he feels what we would feel: pain, fear, and frustration. The authors of science-fiction tales enable us to respond compassionately to their alien creations by supplying them with thoughts and emotions such as we have. Thus, our ability to be compassionate toward another being is related to our ability to attribute to that being a psychological life similar to ours; this is reflected by the fact that we feel compassion most readily and completely toward animals that are closest to us psychologically: we feel more for the sufferings of an ape or a dog than for those of a fish or a spider.

8. Kant, *Metaphysics*, 13.

9. Epictetus, *Manual*, tr. P.E. Matheson. In *Greek and Roman Philosophy after Aristotle* ed. Jason L. Saunders (New York: Free Press, 1966), sec. 3, 134.

10. Kant, *Metaphysics*, 11.

11. David Hume, *An Inquiry Concerning the Principles of Morals*. ed. Charles W. Hendel (Indianapolis: Bobbs-Merrill, 1957) Appendix 1, "Concerning Moral Sentiment," 105.

12. Hume, *Principles of Morals*, 90.

13. Peter Singer, *Practical Ethics* (Cambridge: Cambridge University Press, 1979), 78.

14. Ibid., 83.

15. Ibid., 103.

16. Ibid., 124.

17. Ibid., 73, quoting Anthony Shaw, "Dilemmas of 'Informed Consent' in Children," *New England Journal of Medicine* 289, no. 17 (1973).

18. Ibid., again quoting Shaw.

19. Ibid.

20. In "The Future of Baby Doe," written by Singer and Helga Kuhse for the *New York Review of Books* (March 1, 1984); 17–22, the authors state (22) that

> the unequal worth of human life is really so obvious that we have only to cast off our religious or ideological blinkers to see it as plain as day. If the life of a human being is more valuable than the life of, say, cabbage,

this must be because the human being has qualities like consciousness, rationality, autonomy, and self-awareness which distinguish human beings from cabbages. How then, can we pretend that the life of a human being *with* all these distinctive qualities is of no greater value than the life of a human being who, tragically, has never had and never will have these qualities?

They go on to conclude from this that "any fair and honest solution must recognize that those who will care for the child throughout its life—if it survives—should have the largest say in what steps are taken to keep it alive." Clearly, the outcome of applying this principle in the two cases we have discussed would have been the death of the infant.

21. Singer, *Practical Ethics*, 133.
22. Ibid., 136.
23. Ibid., 148.
24. Ibid., 138.
25. Ibid., 147.
26. Richard Werner, "Abortion: the Moral Status of the Unborn." In *Ethics: Theory and Practice*, eds. Manuel Velasquez and Cynthia Rostankowski (Englewood Cliffs, NJ: Prentice-Hall, 1985), 259. Also in Richard A. Wasserstrom, ed., *Today's Moral Problems*, 2d ed. (New York: MacMillan, 1979), 62.
27. David Hume, *An Inquiry Concerning Human Understanding*, L.A. Selby-Bigge. 3d ed., rev. by P.H. Nidditch (Oxford: Clarendon Press, 1976), sec. 12, Pt. 3, 165.
28. Christina Hoff Sommers, responding to Tooley's advocacy of abortion and infanticide, in "Tooley's Immodest Proposal," *Hastings Center Report* (June 1985): 41–42, argues such a basic obligation.
29. David Hume, "Of Suicide." In *Hume's Ethical Writings*, ed. Alasdair MacIntyre (New York: MacMillan, 1965), 301.
30. Jonathan Glover, "Matters of Life and Death," *New York Review of Books* (May 30, 1985): 20. Glover thinks that this objection can be met satisfactorily by advocates of abortion.
31. Singer, *Practical Ethics*, 154–156.
32. Ibid., 123–124.

# Human Suffering in Comparative Perspective

It is sometimes said that suffering is at once the central puzzle of and the basic reason for religion. While that may be a bit strong, it is surely true that suffering is both an unavoidable point of reference for religious people as well as something mysterious and, frequently, perplexing to them.[1]

We could not imagine any of the world's religions without their preoccupation with the causes of and treatment for affliction, sickness, injury, deprivation, distress, and death. For example, the words of Isaiah in the Old Testament, which capture the heart of prophetic Judaism, only make sense against a background of enduring suffering.

> For behold, I create new heavens and a new earth; . . . I will rejoice in Jerusalem, and be glad in my people; no more shall be heard the sound of weeping and the cry of distress.

> No more shall there be in it an infant that lives but a few days, or an old man who does not fill out his days, for the child shall die a hundred years old.

> They shall not labor in vain, or bear children for calamity; the wolf and lamb shall feed together, the lion shall eat straw like the ox.

> They shall not hurt or destroy in all my holy mountain.[2]

Similarly, St. Paul's famous declaration of Christian confidence in his Letter to the Romans presupposes a profoundly threatening and hostile world, a world fraught with suffering.

Who shall separate us from the love of Christ? Shall tribulation, or distress, or persecution, or famine, or nakedness, or peril, or sword? . . . No, in all these things we are more than conquerors through him who loved us. For I am sure that neither death, nor life, nor angels, nor principalities, nor things present, nor things to come, nor powers, nor height, nor depth, nor anything else in all creation will be able to separate us from the love of God in Christ Jesus, Our Lord.[3]

Although very different in tone and content, Buddha's Four Noble Truths, as enunciated in his first sermon at Benares, organize his teaching around the subject of suffering. The first Noble Truth defines existence as suffering.

The Noble Truth of the origin of suffering is this: It is this thirst which produces re-existence and re-becoming, bound up with passionate greed. It finds fresh delight now here and now there, namely, thirst for sense-pleasures; thirst for existence and becoming.

The Noble Truth of cessation of suffering is this: It is the complete cessation of that very thirst, giving it up, renouncing it, emancipating oneself from it, detaching oneself from it.

The Noble Truth of the path leading to the cessation of suffering is this: It is simply the Noble Eightfold Path, namely right view; right thought; right speech; right action; right livelihood; right effort; right mindfulness; right concentration.[4]

However, if religions are inconceivable apart from the experience of suffering, that experience also creates its own brand of distress, which is the difficulty any religion faces in producing a fully consistent and satisfying explanation of suffering. This difficulty is normally described as the problem of theodicy—of reconciling goodness in the universe with the existence of evil, including suffering.

Although there are undoubtedly quite a number of different theodicies, Max Weber, the German sociologist of religion, called attention to three prominent versions: the dualistic version associated with Zoroastrianism; predestinarian doctrine associated with Calvinist Christianity; and karmic theory associated with Hinduism and Buddhism.[5] In Zoroastrian teaching, two antagonistic gods are posited—a god of goodness and a god of evil—who are conceived of as waging a fierce metaphysical battle, and who are responsible, respectively, for the quotients of prosperity and suffering that exist in the world.

Predestinarianism, as John Calvin worked it out, proposed an all-powerful, good God, author of heaven and earth, who regulates and allots blessings and afflictions, both now and in eternity, according to his mysterious sovereign will. God's will is assumed to be righteous, though in a way that is finally indecipherable from a human point of view.

In karmic theory, reality is so constructed that blessings and afflictions are automatically distributed among human and subhuman beings over a series of reincarnations, according to their righteous or unrighteous behavior as determined by the requirements of *dharma*, or the law of true virtue.

In response, then, to the classical questions of theodicy—as put by the prophet Jeremiah—"Why is it the wicked live so prosperously? Why do the scoundrels enjoy peace?" Zoroastrianism asserts the present, though perhaps provisional, dominance of the evil god. Calvinism invokes the mysterious will of a sovereign, predestining God, and Hinduism and Buddhism trace present miseries to misdeeds in a former life.

The consuming attention that sacred myths and doctrines give to the question of the origins of evil and suffering undoubtedly attests to the commonality and universality of the question. It is of course fashionable nowadays to assert that the concepts, beliefs, and values of different cultural traditions are somehow "incommensurable" or "incomparable," because, as Rorty puts it, "there is nothing deep down inside [human beings] except what we have [from place to place and time to time] put there ourselves."[6]

But when it comes to the matter of human suffering (and probably much more besides), that claim seems manifestly contrary to common sense. The popularity of such a view is, no doubt, simply one more example in the history of human thought of the way certain "brute realities" are overlooked in the name of some theory or other.

I do not suggest that all the world's religions interpret and respond to suffering the same way. The three examples of different theodicies disprove that simple-minded view. But I do contend that there exists a common core to the problem of human suffering, a common core that establishes a baseline for undertaking comparison among different religions. Obviously, unless something is held in common, comparison is impossible.

Part, though not all, of that core is the conscious experience of intense physical pain or of severe physical injury including disablement, disfigurement, or loss of life. It is customary to distinguish between physical pain and suffering, as well as between death or injury and suffering, and there are good reasons for doing that. One might experience intense physical pain and yet be seen to give signs of rejoicing, since that pain signaled the end of paralysis. It seems unlikely we would describe this as "suffering." Or, since the idea of suffering seems ordinarily to suggest conscious experience, it is possible to die unconscious, without suffering. "My grandmother didn't suffer. She died in her sleep," expresses that thought.

Still, there is, I believe, some close connection between the idea of severe physical pain, injury, or death and the idea of suffering. If you have ever experienced intense physical pain or have witnessed someone writhing in pain, it is natural to describe those experiences as examples of suffering. It is very much the right word. It is also quite correct to say, "The quarterback suffered a severe injury in yesterday's game." (Incidentally, I am not sure that when we say that, we have to mean the quarterback was conscious when the injury occurred or even be sure that he will regain consciousness later and know of his injury. The main thing about using the word suffering here may be simply the idea of a severe loss, whatever the victim's state of consciousness was or will be. That is a bit unclear.) It does seem true that the idea of suffering is naturally ascribed to an extreme physical loss, though it may also include the conscious experience of the loss. Both the loss and the awareness would seem to be present when Christians say, "Christ suffered death upon a cross."

## Theoretical Categories of Legitimate Suffering

I do not suggest that basic physical loss, or experiences of such loss, or of severe physical pain, are all there is to our (or anybody else's) notion of suffering. The concept of suffering is, it appears obvious, a rich notion with psychological and spiritual associations, together with all sorts of extended applications as, for example, when we say, "The audience suffered through Little's lecture."

Still, my proposal is that whatever else suffering may mean, the notion is universally built up around this core of basic physical experiences and states. If correct, that yields four truisms about human life: First, human beings everywhere share a deep-seated aversion to severe physical pain, injury, and death, on behalf of themselves and some extended community. Second, all human beings will identify these experiences and states in a common way—they will all, for instance, have a concept of "physical pain" in their language and apply it in a similar way to, say, the experience of unexpectedly being stabbed or breaking a leg. Third, it means that such experiences and states will form a conceptual minimum of the idea of suffering. Fourth, these experiences and states will constitute an unavoidable "negative norm" for organizing social institutions, as well as for thinking about them. In other words, wherever human beings establish societies, they will invariably be concerned to constrain members from inflicting, permitting, or neglecting severe physical pain, injury, or death.

The third and fourth points call for special comment. By "conceptual minimum," I mean that these basic physical experiences and states will function importantly in any theory of suffering. A Buddhist or Christian, for example, will of course contend that "real" suffering is spiritual, not physical. But both will still acknowledge that severe bodily pain, injury, or illness do constitute an indispensable part of what suffering means, and they will propose a way for overcoming such suffering, along with other kinds of affliction, through ultimate spiritual deliverance.

In the Four Noble Truths, Buddhist teaching admits that, among other things, "sickness is suffering, death is suffering," and holds that relief from those conditions can only finally come in the attainment of Nirvana. St. Paul expresses an analogous sentiment when he declares that in Christ's sacrificial act, "Death is swallowed up. O death, where is thy victory? O death, where is thy sting?"

As to the fourth point—that wherever human beings establish societies, they will invariably be concerned to constrain their members in regard to inflicting, permitting, or neglecting severe pain, injury, or death, I have two things in mind: First, societies will in one way or another generate institutions intended to protect members against arbitrary violence such as murder, bodily assault, or physical coercion; or against arbitrary intervention in the treatment of sickness, affliction, or injury.

As a rule, societies will protect their members against arbitrary abuse by authorizing, according to highly solemnized procedures, certain "political-legal" officials to administer "corrective or retributive justice." These officials will be entitled to administer pain, death, and coercion precisely toward the end of preventing, restraining, or punishing arbitrary physical abuse. Furthermore, societies will normally also authorize certain "medical" or "therapeutic" officials to employ carefully certified forms of "care" or "curing," that themselves may require or involve inflicting pain or disablement, or may even lead to loss of life, all in the interest of trying to prevent or overcome greater suffering caused by sickness or injury.

Together with the political-legal and therapeutic regulation of activities relating to pain, injury, and death, there will also be what we might call "pedagogical" regulations. Toward encouraging and, if necessary, enforcing, the initiation of offspring into a community's way of life, certain "educational officials" (frequently including parents) are authorized to inflict certain forms of suffering as a disciplinary measure. One does not have to be Freud, or go the whole way with him, to agree that the process of socialization, of developing "impulse control," is itself an effort of renunciation, of self-denial, that is associated with considerable pain and suffering. It is assumed that discipline is worth it; one "pays the price" so as to avoid that greater suffering to oneself and others that might follow from "raw impulse."

There is one additional sort of action that, though not exactly institutionalized along the lines of the other three, clearly comprises a recurrent type of legitimate suffering. We may call it vicarious suffering of a substitutional or heroic sort. Typically, one interposes oneself as a substitute victim, to protect another from injury or cure another's affliction. The predominance of the heroic theme in cultural traditions bears testimony to its significance.

At the deepest level, then, societies are in the business of organizing suffering. By means of political-legal, therapeutic, and pedagogical institutions, and by means of legitimating vicarious or sacrificial acts on behalf of others, suffering is given a point. It becomes an instrument for restricting, punishing, caring for, or avoiding greater suffering.

Second, and very much related to this, the institution of language, wherever it appears, will come, so to speak, to conceptualize the basic social task of organizing suffering. For one thing, only certain kinds of very stringently regulated reasons will be admitted as excusing or justifying actions that cause or permit pain, injury, coercion, or death. The burden of proof will always fall on the shoulders of those whose actions cause or involve suffering, and full explanations will be required. Generally speaking, it will be necessary to prove that inflicting pain, injury, coercion, or death was called for in order to deter, restrain, or counter arbitrary violence; was necessary to care for a patient threatened by sickness or affliction; was necessary to discipline a recalcitrant inititate; or was necessary to save or aid another in distress.

Above all, purely personal interest or gratification in inflicting pain will never be admitted as a satisfactory explanation or justification. It will simply be no reason at all to say, in defense of stabbing a kinsman or intentionally worsening his ailment, "I happen to like to do it; I find it pleasant." By our account, societies will inevitably regard people who do and say such things as irrational or pathological, for such people simply would not understand the underlying linguistic rules of the game. According to these rules, as we say, only very circumscribed transpersonal or transsubjective reasons could possibly justify causing, permitting, or neglecting suffering. That justification for suffering must be transpersonal or transsubjective—that is, never purely private—is simply another way of indicating the crucially social character of suffering.

The upshot of this, and the interesting part for our purposes, is that the question of human suffering is deeply and commonly embedded in the activity of giving reasons for action. Indeed, though I do not find him altogether congenial company, I would be willing to go part way with Nietzsche and contend, as he does, that the matter of suffering lies at the bottom of all attempts to reason about human existence and conduct. And, as Nietzsche thought, such a proposition brings us back to religion. The idea is that religion, among its other tasks, has the function of providing a comprehensive and ultimate account of the central features of human experience. Therefore, if at least the minimum notion of suffering is as unavoidable, is as much of a brute reality as we suggested, then it follows that religion would have to attend to it. But, if our suggestions are correct, the most intriguing point is that by our analysis of the social and linguistic process of organizing suffering, we have identified some categories that may help us better to understand and compare religious beliefs about suffering. These categories are what we may call four types of legitimate suffering: retributive, therapeutic, pedagogical, and vicarious.

As we saw, these four categories describe the stringently limited sorts of reasons that are commonly acceptable to justify actions and events that involve suffering. Pain, injury, coercion, and death may legitimately be considered as retribution or punishment for violations that themselves involve inflicting pain, injury, coercion, or death. The practice of threatening pain so as to deter violations is simply a variation of the retributive theme. Again, it may be regarded as necessary to inflict a certain amount of suffering on a patient or victim in order to heal. That is therapeutic suffering. Next, some forms of physical suffering may legitimately be considered to be discipline, initiating and instructing the untutored into a community's way of life. That is pedagogical suffering. Finally, vicarious or substitutional suffering can be related to the therapeutic in that someone may assume severe pain, disablement, even death, for the sake of healing the ills or saving the life of someone else. Still, not all vicarious deeds are therapeutic. Heroic action in combat or other violent settings is a rather different way of deflecting suffering from someone else.

I emphasize that the root idea in each of these four types of legitimate suffering is a *reciprocal connection:* In all four, suffering balances suffering (though in different ways). We may infer as a general principle that it takes suffering to justify suffering.

## Legitimate Suffering in Christianity and Buddhism

I want now to try to show the pertinence of these four categories for examining and comparing, briefly, the theories of suffering in Christianity and Buddhism. My basic argument is that, given the way suffering appears to work in shaping human societies, these categories will provide at least an important share of the options for various religious explanations of suffering. One would predict that they will turn up in different traditions, no doubt in different combinations and applications. Let us see, in two cases, whether that is true, and what, therefore, we may learn from the presence of these categories in various traditions.

### Christianity

It is not difficult to show that a retributive understanding is present in the Christian tradition. Lying behind Christianity and the New Testament is the strong Judaic emphasis on retribution, expressed in the Old Testament.

The early Jewish law code, recorded in such books as Leviticus and Exodus, dramatically displays the reciprocal connection we spoke of, according to which suffering in a punitive mode balances suffering that is arbitrarily caused.

> Whoever strikes a man so that he dies shall be put to death. But if he did not lie in wait for him, but God let him fall into his hand, then I will appoint for you a place to which he may flee. But if a man willfully attacks another to kill him treacherously, you shall take him away from my altar, that he may die.[7]

> You shall not afflict any widow or orphan. If you do afflict them, and they cry out to me, I will surely hear their cry; and my wrath will burn, and I will kill you with the sword, and your wives shall become widows and your children fatherless.[8]

> If any harm follows, then you shall give life for life, eye for eye, tooth for tooth, hand for hand, foot for foot, burn for burn, wound for wound, stripe for stripe.[9]

Finally, the same law of retribution lies behind Yahweh's promises to the Israelites, should they not "obey the voice of the Lord . . . or be careful to do all his commandment and his statutes." For such disobedience, "the Lord will smite you with consumption and with fear, inflammation and fiery heat . . . until you perish."[10] Or, as it is summarized in Isaiah, "Tell them, 'Happy is the virtuous man, for he will feed on the fruits of his deeds; Woe to the wicked, evil is on him, He will be treated as his actions deserve.'"[11]

The retributive theme appears abundantly in the New Testament, and, as a consequence, there is much use made of it in the development of Christianity. For example, Isaiah's sentiment, just quoted, is frequently restated in reference to eternal rewards and punishments to be apportioned at the Last Judgment.

> With judgment you pronounce, you will be judged, and the measure you give will be the measure you get.

> The Son of Man will send his angels and they will gather out of his kingdom all causes of sin and all evil-doers, and throw them into the furnace of fire; there they will weep and gnash their teeth.[12]

Moreover, there is to be found in the New Testament, as there is in the Old Testament, mention of a connection between previous misdeeds and sickness or affliction. In the First Letter to the Corinthians, Paul urges all Christians to examine themselves carefully before participating in the Lord's Supper. Because not all had done that, "many of you are weak and ill, and many of you have died."[13] In the Gospels, Jesus frequently cures sick people by saying to them, "Your sins are forgiven you."[14] The assumption is that their sickness or affliction is the result of sins.

But, despite the prominence of retributive suffering in the Old Testament and New Testament, there is obvious dissatisfaction with the idea, at least as a comprehensive explanation for the existence of suffering. There is, for example, Jeremiah's classic lament: "Why is it the wicked live so prosperously? Why do the scoundrels enjoy peace?" The story of Job raises the same problem. Here is a man carefully pictured in the prolog as totally innocent—as "a sound and honest man who feared God and shunned evil," yet he is subjected to catastrophic losses and afflictions. The retributive explanation offered by his three visitors is explicitly rejected in favor of hints, at least, of a pedagogical explanation at the beginning and end of the story. God indulges the mischievous desire of Satan to test the faith of Job, permitting Satan to inflict various forms of suffering on Job. Job passes the test, and, according to the epilog, is rewarded by God for his efforts. This is not strictly retribution, since suffering precedes the benefit, rather than follows sin or misdeed as a penalty. Incidentally, there is also a hint in the epilog that God's reward is to be seen in the context of therapeutic suffering. It is suggested that by absorbing and enduring suffering,

Job conquered suffering, as though he had successfully undergone a painful therapy.

A key perplexity arising out of Jewish experience and reflection is whether the balance of suffering for suffering always works out in a retributive pattern. The New Testament expresses similar disquiet. In the Gospel of Luke, Jesus hears that Pilate has killed some Galileans and mingled their blood with the sacrifices they were offering. "Do you think that these Galileans were worse sinners than all other Galileans because they suffered thus? I tell you, No." Jesus goes on to give the same response in regard to eighteen men who had recently been killed by a falling tower.[15]

We encounter a similar reaction in the Gospel of John, when the disciples want to know why a particular man was born blind. Thinking in retributive terms, they ask whether it was the man's own sin or his parents' that caused the affliction. Jesus responds, "It was not that this man sinned, or his parents, but that the works of God might be made manifest in him."[16] Jesus is moving here from a retributive to a pedagogical explanation. God uses suffering to make a point, to educate or instruct humankind regarding his character and purposes. St. Paul employs the pedagogical theme extensively. Second Corinthians makes use of his own (unnamed) affliction to illustrate that "God's power is made perfect in weakness": "I am content with weaknesses, calamities [and so on], for when I am weak, then I am strong."[17]

A related tension exists in the New Testament between the retributive and the therapeutic theories. In the retributive theory, offenders pay a proportionate amount of suffering as a penalty for the amount of suffering they have caused. The implication is that, by this process, the books can eventually be balanced. Others' suffering is worked off by the offenders' suffering. However, in the therapeutic theory, individuals who are afflicted or in distress are understood to be unable to heal themselves. Patients need the help of another, a "physician," to prescribe and administer a cure. Naturally, the cure entails that patients pay a certain price in suffering if healing is to be achieved. But, above all, the cure is conceived of as a cooperative or social act between physician and patient.

This, of course, is a dominant model in the New Testament. When the Pharisees ask why Jesus eats with tax collectors and sinners, he responds with obvious irony: "Those who are well have no need of a physician, but those who are sick."[18] The response is ironic because it is assumed that only those who know they are sick and in need of a physician's care are truly on the way to being cured. By contrast, those who believe they are well, or are capable of healing themselves by paying whatever penalty they must for past misdeeds, are in fact the ones most in need of a physician's help.

The therapeutic model is obviously exhibited in the extensive reports of Jesus' healing activities throughout the Gospels. There is a deep and interesting ambivalence in these reports of Jesus as physician, as the other who is absolutely requisite to overcome disease and affliction. A total cure depends, of course, on spiritual understanding and achievement in the coming spiritual world, the Kingdom of God that transcends the present world. Still, there is in the Gospels a strong belief in the connection between spiritual and bodily afflictions, and thus between spiritual and bodily healing. The healing mission of Jesus—what we could call his extensive "medical" activity—is, in many ways, a key symbol of the Christian life. According to the Gospel of Matthew, those who care for the sick and the severely distressed will be just the ones who are welcomed into the Kingdom. Caring like a physician for the physically afflicted and deprived, regardless of how they got that way, is the heart of Christian benevolence. No doubt for this reason, it is predicted that the conquest of suffering in the Christian scheme will entail a large amount of physical suffering on the part of the faithful. They are promised persecution of all sorts until the end.[19]

Although, as we said, the vicarious theory is not the same as the therapeutic theory, the two are closely related in the New Testament. According to the use made of the vicarious theory, the physician not only prescribes the therapy for healing, but substitutes himself as the patient, thereby assuming and enduring the pain requisite for cure. As such, this is an extension of the therapeutic model. Here, the physician is at once doctor and patient on behalf of the real patient. This theme is deep within prophetic Judaism as well as early Christianity:

> Surely he has borne our griefs and carried our sorrows;
> Yet we esteemed him stricken, smitten by God and afflicted.
> But he was wounded for our transgressions,
> He was bruised for our iniquities,

Upon him was the chastisement that made us whole
And with his stripes we are healed.[20]

Again, the emphasis on the healing significance of physical distress
is important in Judaism and Christianity. Jesus' reluctance to accept
the pain and suffering that lies in store for him, and his cry of
anguish on the cross underlies that fact. The idea seems to be that
physical suffering must be balanced by physical suffering before
suffering itself can be conquered.

Finally, the vicarious theory is at odds with the retributive
theory in one crucial respect. That suffering must balance suffering
is, as we know, a common feature of all four theories. But what
distinguishes the vicarious explanation is that it heightens the *caring*
motif that is so much a part, also, of the therapeutic understanding.
Ideally, the physician comes to the aid of patient or victim not
because he or she has to, but because of a benevolent concern for
healing the patient's suffering. In one sense, retribution is irrelevant.
The physician simply comes to the aid of those in need, and, in
the vicarious model, goes so far as to pay the price for healing.
That is, of course, the essence of innocent suffering, which is directly
contrary to the retributive scheme.

In certain respects, the history of Christianity (not to mention
the history of Judaism) is simply an exercise in shuffling and recon-
struing these four theories of legitimate suffering. The tension between the retributive and the pedagogical themes that is so clear
in the New Testament continues in the development of Christian
doctrines concerning suffering. For example, Augustine, whose
views on this as on other subjects became so influential, conceived
of suffering in strongly pedagogical terms. For him, affliction, pain,
and distress are, as one might say, a logical necessity. They are
necessary to teach a point about goodness, virtue, and perfection.
Just as we could not have a concept of something's being authentic
unless we also had a concept of something's being counterfeit, nor
could we have a concept "large" without a concept "small," so it
would be logically impossible to have an idea of goodness, virtue,
or perfection without a contrasting notion of evil, vice, or imper-
fection. In Augustine's view, human beings could neither know nor
be good if there were not the realistic prospect of knowing and
being bad and experiencing temptation in that direction; we could
not know and experience release from or conquest over suffering,

if we could not know and experience suffering. To organize life and destiny around the conquest of suffering is to presuppose its necessary existence.

On the other hand, Augustine also made room for a retributive theory that was to beome equally influential in the history of Christianity. He reasoned that when human beings, faced as we were with a realistic choice between good and evil, virtue and vice, freely chose evil and vice, they consequently deserved to be punished, according to retributive requirements, by the afflictions, diseases, and disasters that have historically descended on humankind. Human beings have no one to blame but themselves.

Then again, the therapeutic and vicarious theories find their way into Augustine's thought and dwell there in deep tension with the retributive theory. As we would expect, the idea of Jesus as therapist, and finally as vicarious patient and victim, heightens the emphasis in Augustine and in later Christianity on the *central* legitimacy of unmerited and undeserved suffering. By Christ's sacrificial act—voluntarily absorbing, as it did, severe suffering—the retributive theory was seriously qualified. The fundamental idea is that unretributive suffering, namely suffering that is not exacted as penalty but voluntarily and altruistically confronted and assumed, becomes a strong candidate as the overriding model of legitimate suffering.

## Buddhism

Our general argument, recall, is that in pursuing their basic task of organizing suffering, both institutionally and conceptually, societies will inevitably confront the need to explain and justify suffering. That is in large part what it means to be a society. We further contend that the four categories of legitimate suffering we have identified grow out of and reflect deep and recurrent human responses to a common and universal problem. While the four categories may not be exhaustive, they are central and are likely to feature in one way or another in the philosophical and religious reflection of any cultural tradition.

In considering Buddhism in that light, we are not disappointed. The categories illumine some of the central themes and central tensions of Buddhist thought, and thus provide a useful framework for comparing Christianity and Buddhism (and, if we had time, other traditions as well).

Suffering *(dukkha)*, and overcoming it, lies at the heart of all Buddhist thought and life. To begin with, there is a strong emphasis on retributive suffering in Buddhist thinking, an emphasis firmly oriented toward physical affliction and deprivation. It is impossible to interpret the karmic system, inherited from Hinduism, in any other way. In that system, the world of appearance is governed by inexorable laws of cause and effect. With respect to human action, these laws control the cycle of rebirths to which individuals are subject, so long as they have not fully escaped the world of appearance. Good acts beget good results and bad acts beget bad results in a later rebirth and are measured, in part, in terms of physical blessing or suffering. "Deeds are one's own, . . . beings are heir to deeds."[21] (Note the dramatic similarity between this statement and Isaiah's words, quoted above: "Happy is the virtuous man, for he will feed on the fruits of his deeds; Woe to the wicked, . . . he will be treated as his actions deserve.")

There is the same kind of symmetry between act and consequence that we encountered in the Old Testament material.

> He who destroys the life of any being may, in his next birth, meet death unexpectedly while in the prime of life, even though he is possessed of all the amenities of life, wealth and beauty, like an Adonis.[22]

> Among the karmic results that accrue to the thief are the following: great suffering in an unhappy state for a long period, or, if by virtue of other merits, the thief should be reborn as a man he would lack possessions in this new state. If a man in order to benefit himself is guilty of stealing the property of others, in the next birth he becomes a contemptible beggar clad in dirty rags; with a broken begging vessel in hand, he ever begs his daily bread at the doors of his enemies while suffering a hundred insults.[23]

This clearly retributive interpretation constitutes one sort of theodicy; namely, that present human suffering is explained by individual misdeeds in a previous life. There is presupposed a comprehensive metaphysical distributive system that allocates blessings and afflictions according to just deserts.

But, much as in the Judaic and Christian cases, the retributive system is diminished by a strong competing emphasis on the pedagogical and therapeutic theories of suffering. As in Judaism and Christianity, neither of these latter theories is fully consistent with the retributive pattern. There seems to be a tendency in different traditions eventually to restrict the role of the retributive pattern.

In one sense, Buddhism is nothing more or less than a grand educational system, according to which practitioners progressively graduate from one level of knowledge and wisdom to another. Essential to progress in wisdom is developing the understanding of the universality of suffering, based on human craving and attachment. The only method, ultimately, for overcoming craving and attachment, and thus suffering, is by dissolving the very idea of the craving self. In other words, for the Buddhist, progressively sophisticated analysis of suffering is the salient educational technique for achieving enlightenment. In that sense, suffering is pedagogically indispensable in Buddhism.

It should be noted that the only way the full pedagogical significance of suffering can be appreciated is by directly and consciously confronting suffering, rather than by evading or avoiding it. Suffering must be looked at full in the face—an experience that is itself deeply aversive and painful, at least at the outset. If, in the retributive theory, one suffers because one has caused others to suffer, in the pedagogical model, one conquers suffering by confronting and embracing it. Significantly, true enlightenment delivers one from the retributive karmic system, which is itself based on craving and attachment. The retributive explanation of suffering is thereby eventually reduced in significance.

The caring or benevolent feature so central to the therapeutic theory is abundantly present in Buddhism. The therapeutic explanation is simply an extension of the pedagogical theme. Because of the grip craving and attachment have on human beings, they are not readily capable of educating themselves. They are not just uneducated. They are *afflicted* or sick with ignorance, and consequently need the assistance of an especially enlightened therapist. That role is, of course, primarily played by the Buddha himself. He manifests his care, above all, by providing techniques of enlightenment—therapeutic techniques.

Interestingly enough, those techniques simply further exemplify the point we just made about the importance of confronting and embracing suffering as a means of curing suffering. For example, in the interest of cultivating benevolent attitudes—such as love and compassion for others who suffer—a practitioner at a fairly advanced stage of meditation must call to mind the image of an enemy, of one who inspires anger and resentment. The practitioner should thereby directly confront and acknowledge the suffering that is caused by harboring hostility toward that person. I remember the Dalai Lama's once saying that we ought to learn to thank our enemies for providing an occasion to conquer our aversions toward them. That illustrates the same idea of welcoming suffering associated with enmity, in order to overcome it.

Finally, there is, to be sure, some ambiguity in Buddhism over the role of vicarious suffering, but the idea is by no means totally alien. For one thing, the Bodhisattva ideal, so important in the Mahayana tradition, emphasizes in no uncertain terms that true compassion entails vicarious suffering.

> A Bodhisattva resolves: I take upon myself the burden of all suffering, I am resolved to do so, I will endure it. I do not turn or run away, do not tremble, am not terrified, nor afraid, do not turn back. . . . And why? At all costs I must bear the burdens of all beings. In that I do not follow my own inclinations. I have made the vow to save all beings. All beings I must set free. The whole world of living beings I must rescue, from the terrors of birth, of old age, or sickness, of death and rebirth, of all kinds of moral offence, of all states of woe, of the whole cycle of birth-and-death . . . from all these terrors I must rescue all beings. . . . To the limit of my endurance I will experience in all the states of woe, found in any world system, all the abodes of suffering.[24]

The problem, in Buddhism, raised by the ideal of vicarious suffering is that ultimately every individual must somehow achieve true understanding and true conquest of suffering. Still, that the means for doing that is precisely cultivating benevolent concern for the suffering of others, so that one confronts and endures their suffering as well as one's own, is at the heart of the entire Buddhist message, in Theravada as well as Mahayana. Even in Theravada Buddhism, it is of the greatest importance that the Buddha himself was not content to attain Nirvana for himself alone, but forwent that in the interest of helping to cure all sentient beings of their affliction. There are here the makings of an image of voluntary and substitutional suffering by a thoroughly innocent individual, of paying a price, out of pure benevolence, that others might be healed.

All told, then, there are some amazing parallels between Christianity and Buddhism so far as deploying our four theories is concerned. All four categories are clearly present in both traditions in an important and illuminating way, and they are arranged, up to a point, in a strikingly comparable fashion. Retribution, while very much present in both traditions, is similarly restricted by the other patterns. Moreover, in certain respects, there are interesting parallels between the ways the pedagogical, therapeutic, and vicarious themes work in both traditions.

Still, there are substantial differences. Most significant is the different weight given to physical suffering in Christianity and Buddhism. Although in Christianity, physical suffering is finally overcome spiritually, as it is in Buddhism, there is a prominence ascribed to it that is decidedly absent in Buddhism. Two things in particular exhibit that: the enormous attention given in the Gospels to physical healing as a "sign of the Kingdom," and to the centrality of Jesus' physical suffering and death on a cross. It is as though physical suffering had to be especially and directly accounted for in a way that is not so intense in Buddhism.

Buddhism, by contrast, strongly elevates what we might call pedagogical healing. Enlightenment by instruction and meditation are the obvious focus for overcoming suffering of all sorts, including physical. In other words, physical suffering in Buddhism is for the most part addressed indirectly, though concern with physical healing is not altogether missing. This crucial difference surely accounts for the sharp imbalance between Buddhism and Christianity in respect to the emphasis on physical healing and physical martyrdom.

## Conclusion

Suffering constitutes a common reference point in human life, with its own logic. That logic shows up in comparable ways in different religious systems, as those systems attempt to cope with the difficulty of explaining suffering, or making suffering sufferable.[25] However variable the specific application and interpretation of the retributive, pedagogical, therapeutic, and vicarious theories are, these theories may well be common because they reflect something deep and abiding in the human mind and heart.

If our admittedly preliminary findings have any validity, we may begin to suspect that human beings are not entirely free to think about the problem of suffering in just any way they please. The experience of suffering may be so special that only the suffering, in one way or another, can make it sufferable.

NOTES
1. See John Bowker, *Problems of Suffering in the Religions of the World* (Cambridge: Cambridge University Press, 1977).
2. Isaiah 65:17 ff.
3. Romans 8:35 ff.
4. Cited in Bowker, *Problems of Suffering*, pp. 239–40. Taylor also cites the Four Noble Truths, but with a different translation (pp.19–20).
5. See Max Weber, "The Social Psychology of the World Religions." In *From Max Weber: Essays in Sociology*, eds. H.H. Gerth and C.W. Mills (New York: Oxford University Press, 1958), pp. 275–6 for summary of Weber's views on the subject.
6. Richard Rorty, "Introduction." In *Consequences of Pragmatism* (Minneapolis: University of Minnesota Press, 1982), pp. xlii–xliii.
7. Exodus 21:23–25.
8. Exodus 22:22–24.
9. Exodus 21:23–25.
10. Deuteronomy 28:15, 22 ff.
11. Isaiah 3:10 ff.
12. Matthew 7:2; 13:41–42.
13. I Corinthians 11:28 ff.
14. Luke 5:18 ff.
15. Luke 13:1–5.
16. John 9:1–3.
17. II Corinthians 12:1 ff.
18. Matthew 9:12.
19. See, for example, II Corinthians 4:8 ff.
20. Isaiah 53:4–5.
21. The *Middle Length Sayings*, trans. I.B. Horner Vol.3 (London: Pal. Text Society, 1967), p. 249.
22. Cited in H. Saddhatissa, *Buddhist Ethics: Essence of Buddhism* (New York: George Braziller), p. 89.
23. Ibid., pp. 101–2.
24. Edward Conze, ed., *Buddhist Tests Through The Ages* (New York: Harper and Row, 1964), p. 131. This passage is cited by Taylor, but in a different translation (p. 22).

# Woman's Answer To Job

When human suffering is considered, Job is often taken as the paradigm. His pain was threefold: physical, emotional, and psychical. I will explore the tradition that has grown up around the story of Job and suggest the need for an alternative framework, through which to study the problem of human suffering. This alternative, woman's answer to Job, arises directly out of an ethic of care in contrast to the traditional ethic of justice. Even though ethics of caring are thought by many to be properly associated with women, I must justify my claim that this is woman's answer, and in doing this, I will suggest a special role for the humanities in both health education and medical ethics. Finally, I will use the alternative perspective to take a brief look at some major problems in contemporary health care.

## The Tradition of Job

In the Book of Job we read: "There was a man in the land of Uz, whose name was Job; and that man was perfect and upright, and one that feared God, and eschewed evil."[1] Despite Job's perfection, God allowed Satan to put him to terrible tests of this faith. Job, once rich and well blessed in family life, was undeservedly deprived of everything: His servants were killed; his herds stolen; his seven sons slain by the wind. At last, his body was afflicted from head to foot with "sore boils." On top of all this physical and emotional pain, he suffered the deepest of all pains, psychic or soul pain, as his friends suggested that he must have done something to deserve the evil that was visited on him, and as he struggled to maintain belief in the goodness of God, who willfully permitted him to suffer so. How could God be all-good and at the same time allow Satan to inflict deliberate pain on a just man? For us, the question is why an omniscient deity would thunder on for seventy-one verses, bragging about his omnipotence to a lowly servant long since convinced?[2]

The questions raised in the story of Job have been central in Judeo-Christian theodicies—that is, in attempts to reconcile God and evil. When the problem of evil is stated in terms of a contradiction between an all-good and all-powerful God and the reality of evil, intellectual efforts are directed either to rescuing God from responsibility for evil or to redeeming evil—to explaining that which now appears to be evil in terms of purposes or uses that ultimately produce good. Neither approach encourages us to look at evil as the harm that we do each other by inflicting pain or by failing to relieve it.

Theodicy's thinking has influenced our political, social, and spiritual lives. In both Judaic and Christian traditions, it has counseled us to accept pain as a part of the human condition induced by the Fall, and to find meaning in that suffering. While many human beings continue to be comforted by the views so developed, I will ask whether, perhaps, the comfort is outweighed by the distraction. Might we not ask more powerful questions? Consider, for example, the constraints under which C.S. Lewis labored, when he sought to find meaning in his wife's relentless pain from cancer:

> But is it credible that such extremities of torture should be necessary for us? Well, take your choice. The tortures occur. If they are unnecessary, then there is no God or a bad one. If there is a good God, then these tortures are necessary. For no even moderately good Being could possibly inflict or permit them if they weren't.[3]

In this passage, we see an opening for a line of thought that might recognize a growing God—one in whom good and evil are still both present and only partly differentiated. Indeed Carl Jung claims exactly this about the God of the Old Testament and even suggests that Job was aware of God's shadow side. But Lewis rejects this possibility out of hand. Embracing a conception of God as all-good in spite of the overwhelming evidence against such a view, Lewis believes that God will reward us for our soul-making forbearance and faith. With St. Paul, he affirms "that the sufferings of this present time are not worthy to be compared with the glory that shall be revealed in us."[4] The belief in justice is fundamental and unshakable.

One need not be an atheist or agnostic to identify difficulties in this way of thinking. Even committed theists squirm under Lewis's conclusions. Martin Gardner, for example, says, "This is no solution. It leaves the problem of evil . . . in impenetrable mystery. To any atheist it is a shameful evasion."[5] Still, Lewis's central idea—that evil is somehow redeemed by eventual conversion to good purposes—is the mainspring of Christian theodicy. From this perspective, even Adam's first sin is seen as necessary, and a *felix culpa* or happy fault, since it led ultimately to redemption. "For this reason," says John Hick, "there is no room within the Christian thought-world for the idea of tragedy in any sense that includes the idea of finally *wasted* suffering and goodness."[6]

Although the humanities are steeped in the tradition that seeks meaning in suffering, a rich countertradition in existentialist literature suggests that meaning is created by human beings in their struggle with a universe otherwise devoid of meaning. Suffering in itself has no meaning and is not redeemed simply because it triggers a search for meaning in those who encounter it. Perhaps suffering and goodness are often and finally wasted.

Those of us who urge a look at alternatives do so, not to disparage the dominant religious and ethical tradition but to avoid the alluring distraction it offers. We do not want to look at human suffering and ask only, "What meaning is there in this?" or "What recompense will there be?" Indeed, my great objection to the dominant tradition is that it encourages us to seek justification not only for our own suffering but also for the suffering we inflict on each other. David Little, for example, in a fascinating analysis in Chapter 3 of this volume, identifies several categories of human suffering: retributive, pedagogical, therapeutic, and redemptive. But these are not really categories of suffering; they are categories of reasons we give for inflicting or undergoing pain. If we believe that God teaches us something or cures us of something through pain, then we feel justified in inflicting pain on others in the hope of teaching or curing them. It may, of course, actually be necessary occasionally to cause pain for therapeutic purposes, but the consequence of thinking in this way is failure to challenge the necessity. In the alternative answer suggested by ethics of caring, we do not let the inevitability of suffering lead us into a narrow search for its meaning and justification. Rather, we want to alleviate present suffering, eliminate its causes, and so educate human beings that they will not willfully or negligently induce pain in sentient beings.

To do this, we may need to give up our tenacious belief in a universe administered by a just God, whom we emulate in ethics of justice. Without giving up the search for God and enriched spirituality, we might—as Job did in his unshakable integrity—set an example to whatever gods exist, by our direct and loving care for each other. Working from an ethic of caring, we find immediate cause for action in the pain and delight of those with whom we come into contact; there is no need to distract ourselves in a tangential search for meaning "beyond."

While existentialist literature provides us with an alternative to the notion of meaning built into suffering, it rarely provides us with guidance in caring. In some forms of existentialism, we even find the traditional emphasis on "super-meaning" that distracts us from the central issues. Viktor Frankl, for example, tells us:

> It is self-evident that belief in a super-meaning—whether as a metaphysical concept or in the religious sense of Providence—is of the foremost psychotherapeutic and psychohygienic importance. . . . No great idea can vanish, even if it never reaches public circulation, even if it has been "taken to the grave." In the light of such a law, the drama and tragedy of a man's inner life never have unfolded in vain.[7]

It is understandable that victims of terror and destruction would seek answers in super-meaning—in what Paul Tillich calls an "ultimate concern."[8] But immersion in super-meaning may well lead us away from the obvious tasks that face us as physical human beings. Why should any man, woman, or child have to seek meaning for his or her own life in the horror of the Holocaust? Why should we insist that talent "taken to the grave" is not wasted, that the life so lost is not in vain?

I am more persuaded by the stark honesty of Elie Weisel when he says of his first night in Auschwitz:

> Never shall I forget that night, the first night in camp, which turned my life into one long night, seven times cursed and seven times sealed.

Never shall I forget that smoke. Never shall I forget the little faces of children, whose bodies I saw turned into wreaths of smoke beneath a silent blue sky.

Never shall I forget those flames which consumed my faith forever.

Never shall I forget that nocturnal silence which deprived me, for all eternity, of the desire to live. Never shall I forget those moments which murdered my God and my soul and turned my dreams to dust. Never shall I forget these things, even if I am condemned to live as long as God Himself. Never.[9]

Weisel was fifteen. Who would dare to speak to him of justice? We all know that such things should never have happened and should never happen again. Talk of justice and meaning is out of place in the context of such horror. We need a framework, a theoretical or spiritual perspective, that will keep our hearts and minds directed toward eliminating such moral evil, toward the responsibility of caring for each other. We need a perspective that will help us to find meanings in our relations with fellow human beings, not one that separates us from each other in a quest for super-meaning.

Job, "perfect and upright," was ill-treated by God, and that should be enough to make us wonder whether the God of the Old Testament can guide us in caring for each other. Jung, in his astute and fascinating *Answer to Job*, asks us to consider a developing God, one who was taught a moral lesson by Job, a mere man, and who then answered Job, by becoming a man and sharing the physical, emotional, and psychic suffering of human beings.[10] The dominant theme throughout, however, is still justice—recompense and expiation for evil. In this answer, we find repeated the drama of violence, the holy disregard of intimacy, the deliberate sacrifice of the son, and in the final agonies of Revelation, a new God even more wrathful and terrible than Yahweh. The God described by Jung remains in a titanic struggle to acquire moral control over His own omniscience. What He needs, Jung suggests, is to be rejoined with Sophia, the feminine deity-companion, who will bring wisdom, compassion, and completion to divinity. How might Sophia answer Job? Or should we resist the temptation to seek Sophia and listen, instead, to real women? I wish to leave open here the possibility of a renewed and vital spiritual quest, one in which many women are engaging and in which Jungians are leading the way, but I will not discuss that possibility further now.[11] We will not seek Sophia, but simply woman's answer to Job.

## Why Seek Woman's Answer?

In formulating woman's answer to Job, I will refer to feminine virtues, such as nurturing, mediating, comforting, remaining with, reconciling—in general, caring. Often when such reference is made, someone will protest, "But why call these virtues *feminine?*" One may ask this question for any of several reasons. First, persons unacquainted with the vast literature on women may be unaware that these qualities (and others less favorable) have long been associated with the feminine and thus may suppose that I have simply chosen a set of nice human attributes and claimed them, unfairly, for women.[12] That sort of objection will not hold. As Jane Roland Martin and others have pointed out, some virtues have long been genderized in favor of women; that is, when certain virtues appear in women, they are admired, but the same virtues in men may induce distrust or even scorn.[13] Similarly, virtues genderized in favor of men are not admired in women.

The protestor may be asking a more sophisticated question, may be suggesting that it is time to discard feminine/masculine stereotyping entirely and that this way of talking tends not only to perpetuate stereotypes but to raise animosities. After all, some men are gentle and caring and, surely, some women are not. This is a very important point and some day, indeed, we may be able to pass beyond the feminine/masculine division of virtues. But first, we must courageously claim these virtues as first-class human virtues. For centuries they have been regarded as the virtues of inferior beings—of slaves, subordinates, and women. It cannot be denied that these virtues, together with the Law of Kindness, have been venerated only in the private domain of home and family, whereas masculine virtues, governed by the Law of Justice, have dominated affairs in the public domain. For this very reason, some feminists would like women to reject traditional feminine virtues and cultivate the masculine attributes long associated with first-class citizenship. Other feminists fear such a move and worry that the very best human attributes may thus be lost—and with them the hope for human survival. These feminists are likely to resent what they see as male attempts to co-opt feminine virtues now that they have become attractive. I think we will have to live generously through a period in which strong women will claim these virtues as their own, as part of a long and hard-earned heritage. We will continue to suggest that these valuable qualities are better nourished through feminine experience than through masculine and, therefore, if men truly admire and wish to adopt them, it will be necessary to transform our educational system, our religious frameworks and, in general, our sociopolitical ways of thinking so that both feminine and masculine experiences are optimally represented in our institutions.

Some protestors will remain unsatisfied at this point. They will argue that the best male leaders have advocated and even modeled the virtues under discussion. Human beings have just not followed what Jesus, Gandhi, and Martin Luther King have preached. So what reason have we to suppose that people will listen to women? There is a grave misunderstanding here. Beautiful as the messages and lives of these men were, there was still something vital missing in them. All of them showed dramatic weaknesses in the morality of intimacy—in their dealings with those closest to them. As Carol Gilligan puts it, referring to Erik Erikson's studies of Gandhi and King, "while the relationship between self and society is achieved in magnificent articulation, both men are compromised in their capacity for intimacy and live at great personal distance from others."[14]

Now the objection may be raised that I ask too much. After all, every human being has frailties, and men who are striving to achieve world-embracing systems are bound to seem a bit aloof and different from the rest of us. But it is not the presence of small weaknesses that concerns us. We are concerned, rather, with the effects on both preachers and listeners of continued attempts to construct universal, abstract, and unattainable systems of moral thought. In all these cases, the struggle for moral perfection in followers has led to irruptions of behavior directly contraindicated by the guiding abstract system. This is the phenomenon Jung called "enantiodromia," in which the total striving for something at one pole of an oppositional pair—say goodness—induces a dangerous flow of repressed energy to the opposite pole, with the result that evil breaks out violently.[15] It is because this has happened repeatedly in cultures governed by the great masculine systems that many of us feel it is time to try transplanting the virtues of the private domain into the public domain. It is time to elevate the Law of Kindness to a position of equality with the Law of Justice. This is where women's experience should be invaluable.

Having answered the question, why should we seek woman's response to Job, I will attempt to describe that response. Woman's answer to Job is given in her personal, caring presence. She says, "I am here. Let me help you." She does not judge, or condemn, or dominate with commands. She does not turn his attention (or her own) away from the human beings who are his present help and solace, toward some eternal principle that he should grasp in order to be justified. She feeds him and the friends who visit him. She begs them not to fight among themselves, and she counsels against seeking vengeance on the thieves and marauders. She shows them how they can be reconciled not to one man's awful fate but to each other and, hence, achieve a better common fate. Her ontology is one of relation, not of individual and totally separate beings.

## In the Spirit of Woman's Answer

Now, I will explore the application of this relational mode of thinking and being in the world. Radical new procedures and innovative social thought are changing the field of health and medicine dramatically. With the possible exception of war and peace, no other field stands in greater need of rigorous and imaginative ethical thinking. It is no longer reasonable to rely on old adages, such as Job's "The lord gave and the lord hath taken away."[16] Increasingly, human beings are instrumentally and responsibly involved in both giving and taking away. How shall we think as we take on these responsibilities?

In the remainder of this chapter, I want to do two things: (1) to illustrate the relational mode of thinking in a discussion of abortion; and (2) to talk directly about the possible contributions of the humanities to the ethical thinking that must be undertaken by the caring professions. Please keep in mind that this method intentionally avoids accusations of wrong or claims to be right. It does not draw on eternal principles or rigid rules. It does not attempt to reconcile us with a spiritual entity. Most important, it makes no attempt to draw lines of opposition but, rather, seeks to keep us in sensitive conversation with each other as we search for solutions that enhance the quality of life and consciousness.

In *Caring*, I discussed abortion from a relational perspective.[17] My argument focused on response, not on rights. I tried to show how caring people think and feel their way through situations of conflict by considering their relations to others and the quality of human response present or potential in each of the participants.

Operating under the guidance of an ethic of caring, we are not likely to find abortion in general either right or wrong. We shall have to inquire into individual cases. An incipient embryo is an information speck—a set of controlling instructions for a future human being. Many of these specks are created and flushed away without their creators' awareness. From the view developed here, the information speck is an information speck; it has no given sanctity. There should be no concern over the waste of "human tissue," since nature herself is wildly prolific, even profligate. The one caring is concerned not with human tissue but with human consciousness—with pain, delight, hope, fear, entreaty, and response.

But suppose the information speck is mine, and I am aware of it. This child-to-be is the product of love between a man deeply cared for and me. Will the child have his eyes or mine? His stature or mine? Our joint love of mathematics or his love of mechanics or my love of language? This is not just an information speck; it is endowed with prior love and current knowledge. It is not sacred, but I—humbly, not presumptuously—confer sacredness upon it. I cannot, will not destroy it. It is joined to loved others through formal chains of caring. It is linked to the inner circle in a clearly defined way. I might wish that I were not pregnant, but I cannot destroy this known and potentially loved person-to-be. There is already relation albeit indirect and formal. My decision is an ethical one born of natural caring.

But suppose, now, that my beloved child has grown up; it is she who is pregnant and considering abortion. She is not sure of the love between herself and the man. She is miserably worried about her economic and emotional future. I might like to convey sanctity on this information speck; but I am not God—only mother to this suffering, cared for one. It is she who is conscious and in pain, and I, as one caring, move to relieve the pain. This information speck is an information speck and that is all. There is no formal relation, given the breakdown between husband and wife, and with the embryo, there is no present relation; the possibility of future relation—while not absent, surely—is uncertain. But what of this possibility for growing response? Must we not consider it? We must indeed. As the embryo becomes a fetus and, growing daily, becomes more nearly capable of response as a cared for being, our obligation grows from a nagging uncertainty—an "I must if I wish"—to an utter conviction that we must meet this small other as caring people.[18]

If we had to translate this line of thinking into a legal position, we would find ourselves roughly in accord with the Supreme Court pronouncement: Early abortions should be freely available; later ones should be subjected to medical and external ethical scrutiny. Thus, an ethic of relation and response may lead us to the same general conclusion as one of rights and justice. But the argument over rights is by no means finished. Those who would argue from this perspective must consider the rights of the fetus, and once this line of argument is under way, we are again distracted from the present problem of conscious human suffering to abstract analytical problems, such as: When does life begin? What is a person? Whose rights should prevail and why? Those arguing for the rights of women to control their own bodies will go to extremes in trying to show that the fetus is merely a bit of tissue; those advocating the rights of unborn children will insist on an *a priori* sanctity of life for every fertilized cell. Nothing in an ethic of rights, even if it is sensitive to conscious human suffering, directs us to love and care for each other even as we argue the issues.

An ethic of caring, however, suggests that our problem is not entirely solved when we arrive at a decision that is compassionately justified in the eyes of a reflective majority. We still must deal with those who believe passionately that abortion is murder. Some of you may belong to this group, and so we have a common problem every bit as important as the first problem: How shall we talk to each other? How can we enter into or maintain a caring relation with each other even though we differ dramatically on a fundamental question of value?

In our answers to these questions—or more often in our failure even to ask the questions—we have made many errors. We have turned our backs on each other, each side considering the other to be hopelessly deficient in either morality or logic or both. First, then, we must summon the will to bear with each other, to continue in conversation. But, also, we must clean up our own thinking and articulate our positions honestly. The point that I want to make here is that we cannot get at fundamental moral issues if we persist in making logical errors that cloud our true positions and lead us into inauthenticity. By way of illustration, I will consider Geraldine Ferraro's position on abortion. On the surface her position looks very like mine; she rejects abortion for herself but allows others to make their own decisions. But our positions are really not at all alike. Her personal rejection of abortion is grounded in a moral principle and not, as mine was, in the recognition of love, support, and natural caring. My decision for myself could have been different, if my life situation had been different. An ethic of caring makes it logically valid for A to decide X, and B to decide not-X, if both have reflected on their situations and considered the appropriate factors of relation and response. But Ferraro is caught in a logical error. She admits to belief in a principle that, if accepted, must by its very nature be binding on everyone if it is on anyone. In the traditional ethic to which her church subscribes, moral precepts must be universalizable. Thus, she has placed herself in the untenable position of saying, in effect, that she believes abortion to be an immoral act forbidden by God and that at the same time she also believes that people should have the legal right to commit this immoral act. She could, of course, have taken a strictly legal position affirming the separation of church and state; she would, then, have been committed to administering a law she thought to be immoral, but she would also have been committed to trying to change it. Another alternative, one perhaps most consistent with Ferraro's position, is to accept the Church's position as a "teaching of the Church" rather than a moral pronouncement, and thus to find herself bound by it while others are free to decide the question under their own spiritual or ethical guidance. This position induces spiritual agony, however, because it stands in personal opposition to the Church's official doctrine.

Can philosophical thinking guide people in such soul-trying predicaments? Does accepting such guidance demand an end to religious faith and a frank allegiance to some form of humanism? Some of us have, of course, made this decision, but I do not think it is entailed or necessitated by the prior decision to think reflectively. I do think this prior decision commits us to thinking reflectively about our religious beliefs and to quit hiding behind what we call "respect" for alternative religious views in our refusal to discuss religious matters in public. Positions worthy of respect can withstand the rigors of public debate.

As we begin to talk with each other about our religious beliefs, I think we will find that believers have many different gods, and that even those who believe in no gods often confess a psychic longing that might be called "religious." The humanities can help us enormously in conducting this conversation. Carl Jung urged us to think of God as a psychic reality, an archetype, that can manifest itself in a variety of ways—that is, in a multiplicity of gods, none of which in itself can be God.[19] Julian Jaynes suggests that human beings once stood eye-to-eye with their gods in direct and unreflective communion.[20] Merlin Stone convincingly documents her claim that the God before Yahweh was a woman.[21] Increasingly, feminists (along with such thoughtful theists as Martin Gardner) are boldly rejecting the god of the Pentateuch. We simply will no longer accept a god who orders his followers to destroy other human beings.[22]

When we accept that a multiplicity of gods dwell among us, I think we humanists and near-humanists can better understand the rage of fundamentalists when we say something of this sort to them: "Look, I believe in the same God you do, but I'm smarter and better educated, and you simply have Him all wrong." Who would not respond angrily to such an attitude? It might be better to approach the fundamentalist like this (after listening): "Ah, so that is what your god commands. Now I understand your decision. But—here, sit down a minute—let me tell you about *my* god." In all of these discussions, we behave as though in a family; we extend the caring behaviors and ways of thinking long associated with the private domain into the domain of public thinking and acting.

Now, why must the caring professions be concerned with such odd conversations? Our first answer is, of course, that we must simply because we are the *caring* professions and are, therefore, by definition, concerned with the physical, emotional, and psychic care of our clients. But the second answer is that we must broaden our vision if we are to have any chance at all to cope with an era of new ethical problems. How are we to conduct the genetic research that will surely influence our own evolution? Should we learn how to help people to die as well as to live? Should we actually provide the means for people to die, if they or their families and counselors choose death in preference to intolerable existence? Should we fear or welcome "fabricated man"?[23] It may be theoretically possible to solve our moral problems within clear, abstract ethical theories of justice, but it is not *practically* possible to do so. In the intense passions of real life, we will have to acknowledge and work with the sources of those passions. As traditional formulas fail—and they must because they do not even contain the variables that are now being created—we will have to turn receptively and constructively to each other to find new guidance.

Here I see the humanities useful more as a method than as a fixed heritage, for they too will have to change. Recently, Ernle Young noted that a whole generation of aspiring medical students "had to forsake a broad education in the humanities—where they might have learned some important values—concentrating instead on what is euphemistically known as premedical education."[24] While agreeing with the spirit of Young's remarks, I would modify his claim on values, saying instead that students of the humanities might learn how to approach questions of value, how to recognize fundamental values, how to talk with people about such issues, and how feelings are expressed in matters of value.

Before closing, I want to discuss another problem for the caring professions—one to which Dean Young also alluded in his talk on medical integrity. He said, "The vast majority of those who enter medicine did so because they wanted to benefit their fellow human beings and leave their world a little better for having lived and worked in it."[25] But this idealism, he pointed out, fades under inordinate pressures, and integrity is often lost along with the naive ideals of youth. The caring professions are today in sore need of someone to care for them. Physicians, nurses, teachers, social workers, technicians, and helpers all risk burnout in professions that require them to give unceasingly, and more and more often these valuable people become caught up in battles for their own "rights."

Here again, I think, an ethic of caring and response may prove more useful than one of justice and rights. Consider one huge problem: malpractice suits. How might we approach this problem from a caring perspective? Caring physicians want to respond openly, helpfully, and individually to their patients. They do not want to answer by formula or out of fear for their own livelihood. Physicians ought not to have to "read patients their rights," so to speak, before every procedure and thus risk frightening some who are quite willing to proceed without the latest statistics. Physicians, nurses, and other health workers might consider entering into voluntary alliances with communities of patients. Patients would agree not to sue; health-care workers would charge lower rates. The money saved would provide a community resource to care for the unfortunate. No "damages" would be paid, but steady, appropriate care and *caring* would be provided. Everyone in the voluntary community would pledge some time and, perhaps, part of some other valuable resource. Under such an arrangement, an environment of trust would be constructed, and people would be able to talk to each other again. (Since writing this, I have been informed that such discussions are under way in some medical communities, and that lawyers, too, are considering the construction of communities in which the focus of their work would switch from adversarial relations and litigation to reconciliation and interpretation.)

Under an ethic of caring, we look for smaller, more personal, more family-like solutions to the problems of human living. This does not preclude an interest in rigorously developing and applying theories, but our new theories must come out of and be designed to serve actual human living. As Jean Watson observed in her theoretical work on nursing, "We need to develop methods that retain the human context and allow for advancement of knowledge about the lived world of human experience."[26] Ethics of justice tend toward higher and higher levels of abstraction, impersonal decision-making, and continual contests for competing rights. Ethics of caring, in contrast, tie us to the people we serve, not to the rules through which we serve them.

Conclusion

I have tried to show how an ethic of response and caring seeks to respond directly to the sufferer and to those related to him. I have suggested that education in the humanities can contribute to education in health sciences, not only in the traditional ways, but more importantly, in the gift of method. The humanities are being broadened and deepened by the challenge of feminism, and their traditional authority in describing the human condition will be further strengthened by the inclusion of feminine thinking. It may be time to use this thinking to challenge the gods—as technology and science have always done—but not in a struggle for power and control. Rather, our challenge is aimed toward cooperation and harmony. It is a courageous affirmation that, come what may, we will go on caring for each other.

NOTES
1.  Job 1:1.
2.  This question is raised by Carl G. Jung in *Answer to Job*, tr. R.F.C. Hull (Princeton, NJ: Princeton University Press, 1973), 16.
3.  C.S. Lewis, *A Grief Observed* (Toronto, New York, and London: Bantam, 1976), 50.
4.  C.S. Lewis, *The Problem of Pain* (New York: Macmillan, 1962), 144. Lewis quotes from Romans 8:18.
5.  Martin Gardner, *The Whys of a Philosophical Scrivener* (New York: Quill, 1983), 253.
6.  John Hick, *Evil and the God of Love* (London: Macmillan, 1966), 280. The *felix culpa* appears in the Roman Missal, in *Exultet* to be sung on Easter Eve. It is sometimes attributed to St. Augustine.
7.  Viktor Frankl, *The Doctor and the Soul* (New York: Alfred A. Knopf, 1968), 33.
8.  Paul Tillich, *The Courage to Be* (New Haven, CT: Yale University Press, 1952).
9.  Elie Weisel, *Night* (New York: Hill and Wang, 1960), 43–44.
10. Jung, of course, is not the only thinker to suggest a developing God. See also Alfred North Whitehead, *Process and Reality* (Cambridge: Cambridge University Press, 1929); and Charles Hartshorne, *The Logic of Perfection* (Lasalle, IL: Open Court, 1962). "Process theologies" are currently alive in Catholicism and Judaism as well as in some forms of Protestantism.
11. But, see James Hillman, *Re-Visioning Psychology* (New York: Harper and Row, 1975); Christine Downing, *The Goddess* (New York: Crossroad, 1984); Naomi Goldenberg, *Changing of the Gods* (Boston: Beacon, 1979); Jean

Shinoda Bolen, *Goddesses in Everywoman* (San Francisco: Harper and Row, 1984).

12. See, for example, any of a vast array of Jungians: M. Esther Harding, *Woman's Mysteries* (New York: Harper and Row, 1971); Erich Neumann, *The Great Mother* (Princeton, NJ: Princeton University Press, 1955); Downing, *The Goddess*; Irene Claremont de Castillejo, *Knowing Woman* (New York: Harper and Row, 1974); Bolen, *Goddesses in Everywoman*; Jung, *Answer to Job*.

13. See Jane Roland Martin, *Reclaiming a Conversation* (New Haven, CT: Yale University Press, 1985).

14. Carol Gilligan, *In a Different Voice* (Cambridge, MA: Harvard University Press, 1982), 155.

15. See Jung, *Answer To Job*, in which he psychoanalyzes John the Apocalyptist.

16. Job 1:21.

17. Nel Noddings, *Caring: A Feminine Approach to Ethics and Moral Education* (Berkeley: California University Press, 1984).

18. Ibid., 87–88.

19. On the psychic reality of God, see Jung, *Answer To Job*.

20. Julian Jaynes, *The Origin of Consciousness in the Breakdown of the Bicameral Mind* (Princeton, NJ: Princeton University Press, 1982).

21. Merlin Stone, *When God Was A Woman* (San Diego: Harcourt Brace Jovanovich, 1976).

22. See Nel Noddings, "A Feminine Approach to Ethics." Working Paper 18 (Stanford, CA: Stanford University Center for Research on Women, 1985).

23. See the discussion in Paul Ramsey, *Fabricated Man* (New Haven and London: Yale University Press, 1970).

24. Ernle Young, in an address to John S. Knight fellows, Stanford University Department of Communication, July 9, 1985.

25. Ibid.

26. Jean Watson, *Nursing: Human Science and Human Care* (Norwalk, CT: Appleton-Century-Crofts, 1985), 2.

FREDRICK R. ABRAMS, M.D.

# Medical-Ethical Perspectives on Human Suffering

Is there anything that we currently label a unique medical ethic? Values differ substantially from culture to culture, and doctors have more in common with fellow citizens of their own culture than with doctors from another culture. In Western cultures, there appear two types of medical ethics: one paternalistic (with older roots), and the other contractual (with more modern roots). Healing as the core of a medical ethic falls short; relief of suffering must be considered equally critical. I will discuss what could be a universal medical ethic in a culture such as ours, where self-determination is valued. Finally, I will discuss three dilemmas: (1) truth-telling and suffering from uncertainty; (2) informed consent and suffering from helplessness; and (3) the dilemmas that arise from death and dying, and the "slippery slope" on which killing and "letting die" are precariously distinguished.

Ethics, morals, and values are words whose definitions are constantly disputed. It is helpful to find a common starting place; I will delineate the relationship I will be using among ethics, morals, and values. *Ethics* is defined as a set of general rules to determine what is good and what is bad. Using these rules, personal *moral* judgments are derived, based on the *values* of the particular cultural environment we are considering.

Currently, there is no single and unique medical ethic that can be used to develop a medical-ethical perspective on human suffering. To borrow a phrase from Dr. Edmund Pellegrino, "Medicine suffers from an abundance of means and a poverty of ends." For example, American physicians practice within a value framework like that of other American citizens, and with a substantial element of patient self-determination, while Soviet physicians value community, as do most Soviet citizens. The Soviet Oath of 1971 states: "Treatment is to be according to the principles of Communist morality. Responsibility is to the people and to the Soviet government and the interests of society."

Certainly, physicians have some values in common. In either country, doctors are dedicated to healing, but in the USSR they might wish to heal mental aberration evidenced by political dissent, while in the United States they might treat mental aberration characterized by socially unacceptable sexual behavior. Within our culture, where the political model is secular and pluralistic (a relatively recent historical development of the separation of church and state, and freedom from a single dominant moral authority), a physician turns to his or her personal morality when facing professional decisions about such critical issues as dying, abortion, or truth-telling, or a patient's role in his or her own care. The legacy of medicine, from the time it began as a craft of healing, has been a variety of codes of behavior. The mystical aspects of healing and its religious overtones permeate codes and persist even in modern attempts to identify an ethic unique to medicine.

An overriding tension in modern medical practice arises between beneficence—the duty to do good—and autonomy—the patient's right of self-determination. Robert Veatch, in his book *A Theory of Medical Ethics*, has characterized the two principles as the Hippocratic tradition and historically more recent "convenantal" tradition. The Hippocratic Oath is attributed to the relatively insignificant Pythagorean cult and was written centuries after Hippocrates' death. It contains the essence of the traditional paternal beneficence: "I will apply . . . measures for the benefit of the sick according to my ability and judgment; I will keep them free from harm and injustice." In the remainder of the oath, the physician assumes the role of the concerned parent, doing for his child what he, the physician, deems best. It is the oldest known Western tradition, bolstered by the sometimes presumed and sometimes real difference in power, knowledge, or social status between the physician and the patient. It is a code of individuals, dealing only with the doctor and patient and having no significant consideration for the larger society. Veatch characterizes the alternative medical ethic as convenantal; note he uses a term steeped in theological overtones.

The relationship between doctor and patient in this model is contractual. It is a fiduciary relationship in which it is acknowledged that one of the contractors has special knowledge and agrees to use it on behalf of the other. It is a contract of utility or consequences, a social rather than individual concept, but in Veatch's recommended model, the utilitarian contract is tempered by several constraints. The physician is obligated to: (1) keep promises; (2) respect the patient's autonomy; (3) be honest; (4) avoid killing; and (5) be just in dealings. In our kind of open, pluralistic society, this model appeals to our value system. It is the model that could be anticipated from our political and social evolution, from early authoritarianism to the more recent emphasis on self-determination.

Pellegrino, in his book *A Philosophical Basis of Medical Practice*, made a noteworthy attempt to derive a philosophy unique to medicine and drew certain conclusions that appear to be universally true: Health is so fundamental that loss of it threatens our integrity and disrupts our function; this leads us to fundamental questions about the meaning of existence and death; medicine implies a unique relationship between people, and its philosophy is not reducible to biology, physics, chemistry, and psychology. Pellegrino offers some medical axioms that also appear to be cross-cultural universals: (1) Do no harm; (2) respect the vulnerability of the patient (this is certainly beneficent but it might be disguised paternalism); and (3) treat patients as human beings of equal worth. Perhaps most important, he states that the central thrust of medicine is an ethic of healing. I agree with Pellegrino that healing (the root meaning is "making whole") is a necessary goal, but our knowledge and ability is imperfect, and we often fall short of this desired end. As a practical matter, the goal of healing is necessary but not sufficient. By itself, it falls short of being the core of an universal medical ethic.

Doctors need to be reminded about suffering, for that is why medical attention is sought. Pain and suffering are often paired but need to be considered separately by the good physician. Pain is a physiological phenomenon; suffering is a psychological phenomenon. An injured finger may be the cause of delight to a construction worker who gets four weeks vacation with pay but may cause the most severe suffering to a concert violinist, who finds his *raison d'être* threatened. Relief of suffering must be considered at least of equal merit as a goal for the physician. In fact, it may be more universally achievable than is healing. Just as the law finds it easier to prescribe unacceptable actions than to prescribe all actions that society agrees are acceptable, so also it is easier to agree on what most people would prefer to avoid than on what they desire, regarding their health.

Medicine has been characterized as an art and as a science. As the scientific foundation grew, more focus was placed on the illness itself, and less on the bearer of the illness. It is as if medicine had come full circle and returned to the era when disease had to be exorcised by a contest of wills between the priest-doctor and the devil-disease. I suggest that the appropriate model for the medical ethic ought to be a therapeutic alliance of the patient and doctor, directed toward healing but tempered by the need for relief of suffering. If I were to paint a picture of this concept, I would paint it as a lever with the fulcrum in the middle. On one end of the lever would be "healing," on the other end would be "relief of suffering." Where these goals conflict, the informed patient must be expected and permitted to make the decision as to how the balance should tilt. How the lever tilted would depend on where the patient set the fulcrum, knowing that there was a likelihood that it might have to be moved many times depending on diagnosis, treatment, and prognosis. Having circuitously arrived at the core of my argument, I turn to the very specific, discussing three areas of medical intervention where ethical dilemmas arise and suggesting means of dealing with them to minimize suffering.

## Truth Telling and Uncertainty

In *The Death of Ivan Illych*, Tolstoy tells us:

> What tormented Ivan Illych most was the deception, the lie which for some reason they all accepted, that he was not dying but simply ill. . . . After prolonged suffering he wished most of all (though he would have been ashamed to confess it) for someone to pity him as a sick child is pitied. He longed to be petted and comforted."

Ivan could not confess it, because, like many patients, he participated in the charade, knowing he was dying yet hoping he was somehow wrong. Neither the patient nor the caretaker can summon the courage to break the tenuous balance that enables him to avoid facing a culturally unacceptable truth. If there is nothing in their belief system that accepts death as part of life, death becomes unthinkable and unspeakable. There is now occurring an evolution away from deception and toward truth-telling in medicine. It is not difficult to explain why this has been such a difficult struggle and one that still goes on.

In an era when there was precious little effective treatment for any serious ailment, and a physician's reputation depended more on his ability to prognosticate (and therefore to know which cases to refuse), there were two principle reasons for deception. First, there was concern about worsening the outcome; physicians were well aware of the effect of negative suggestion or prediction of poor outcome. Decorum, in the Hippocratic corpus, directs the physician, "Reveal nothing . . . many patients have taken a turn for the worse."[5] A code of India, dated about A.D. 100, instructs the physician, "Even knowing the patient's span of life has come to its close, it shall not be mentioned by you if, when done, it would cause shock to the patient or to others." Also recognized was the positive placebo effect (placebo translates literally from the Latin, "I shall please"). Isaac Israeli, a ninth-century physician, instructed, "Reassure the patient and declare his safety even though you may not be certain of it, for by this you will strengthen his nature."

The placebo effect is well known. When any new medicine is tested against a placebo (an inactive substance that should, physiologically, have no positive or negative effect), about 35 percent of patients will be affected by it. Many will improve, but, equally interesting, many will have such side effects as nausea, skin rash, diarrhea, or vertigo. It is easy to see how an authority figure can, simply by word or manner, influence the course of disease. But of course, a physician does not have to deceive to use this power on behalf of the patient.

The second reason for deception arose from the Hippocratic tradition of parentalism, best characterized by a quote from Cicero: "A forewarning of evil is justified only when a means of escape is joined to the warning." Both of these positions are still argued by modern physicians. Nonetheless, telling the truth is, for modern caretakers, difficult to avoid. Patients are sophisticated and often elicit a pledge of no-holds-barred honesty before undergoing diagnostic procedures. Furthermore, there are treatments for malignancies that hold out hope for cure, but they are potent treatments with potent side effects. No one would accept the hazards and discomforts without the knowledge that the treatment was the only hope for survival.

What can be said of the second deception: not speaking of an evil that cannot be avoided? Arguments, pro and con, began even in ancient Greece, for Celsus advised that relatives be informed of a poor prognosis (probably at least to protect the physician's reputation) and Ctesias more directly advised patients that since they were facing danger, a will should be made.

The modern argument for truth was epitomized by the physician Richard Cabot in his 1909 essay, *The Use of Truth and Falsehood in Medicine*: "If it is generally accepted that doctors lie, who will trust them?" The thrust of his article was that lying may be acceptable for those who say "Let the buyer beware" or "Business is business," but it is not a good ethic for those whose stock in trade is trust. If a doctor's character is questioned, it would not be unreasonable to question the motivation of his recommendations for treatment, from which he might benefit financially. Trust is critical for the medical enterprise, and patients must never have reason to question whether they have been told the truth or for whose benefit the doctor is prescribing.

If the medical ethic stops at healing, the debate rages on. But, if equally at its core is relief of suffering, no dilemmas need remain. By educating the physician, there is much that can be offered the gravely ill patient. Ours is a death-denying culture, and doctors come from this same society. Some of them studied medicine because of their own fear of death. Some doctors do not wish to talk about death or confront a dying patient or the patient's family, because the doctor considers failure to cure to be a personal failure. The doctor avoids contact with the patient, and sometimes so does the hospital staff, because of fear of inadvertently exposing the truth; everyone becomes evasive. The patient feels abandoned when the doctor, who usually made rounds twice daily, suddenly drops out of sight for days at a time. The patient begins to fear, and the uncertainty exacerbates the fear. The doctor must be made aware of how important a role he or she can continue to play if these faulty assumptions of guilt can be overcome.

Before the patient cares *what* we know, he must know that we care. Suffering can be relieved, by not abandoning the patient when science fails. Although no more can be done against the disease, much more can be done for the patient. Truth-telling relieves the sufferer of uncertainty and mistrust; a physician whose ethic goes beyond healing, when curing is no longer possible, and emphasizes caring in the face of an unpleasant truth, continues to render valuable service in alleviating suffering.

## Informed Consent and Feelings of Helplessness

I need not dwell on the indignities imposed on patients when they enter the hospital. They are not unlike military recruits, whose heads are shaved and who are given uniforms. Hospital uniforms, hospital routines, inflexible schedules smack of the same principle. The very word, uniform, indicates the loss of individuality. With that, the patient loses his autonomy, as he is encouraged to submit to an all-knowing authority promising to care for his every need, if he will only submit as a child to a parent. But, our culture cherishes individuality and self-determination; there is inherent tension in this situation. Our society has rebelled against this imposition, using the courts to uphold patient autonomy.

This was not always the case. Early American court decisions upheld the "father knows best" principle. There is a case documented in the medical literature in the early part of this century where a patient was offered an operation for cataracts. Being prudent, he consented to surgery on one eye only, to which the physician agreed. Under anesthetic, both cataracts were operated on, and, as a consequence, the patient became blind in both eyes. He sued the physician but lost his case. There was ample testimony, and no dispute that the operation was performed correctly and without negligence. The fact was that the doctor's judgment concerning the choice of operating on both eyes prevailed, despite the patient's prudent request that only one be done.

A significant shift began with the case of Schloendorff v. the

Society of New York Hospital in 1914. Chief Justice Benjamin Cardozo stipulated: "Every human being of adult years and sound mind has the right to determine what shall be done with his own body and a surgeon who performs an operation without his patient's consent commits an assault." This led the way for consent for surgery being a necessary prerequisite.

In 1960, the case of Natanson v. Kline further underscored the principle of informed consent when Justice Schroeder stated, "A doctor may well believe that an operation or form of treatment is desirable or necessary, but the law does not permit him to substitute his own judgment for that of the patient by any artifice or deception." In 1972, a far-reaching decision, Canterbury v. Spence, pushed consent even further by deviating from the usual professional standard that had been used for consent and saying instead, "Respect for the patient's right of self-determination . . . demands a standard set by law for physicians, rather than one physicians may or may not impose on themselves." This opposed the principle of "therapeutic privilege," which is an argument still relied on and which sets a professional standard for distinguishing what ought to be said and what ought not, "where disclosure . . . would seriously jeopardize the recovery of an unstable, temperamental, or severely depressed patient." That there is still resistance from the profession can be inferred from the titles of articles written by physicians in response to these decisions, such as "The Myth of Informed Consent," by Ravitch, "Malpractice and Informed Consent: A Legal Ploy," by DeLees, "The Fiction of Informed Consent," by Laforet, and "Terrified Consent," by Coleman.

The difference between English and American medical systems and jurisprudence is graphically illustrated in a recently decided case in England, denying the legal principle of informed consent. It is interesting to note that fewer than 1,000 malpractice cases were filed in England the year that this case was filed. Sidaway v. the Board of Governors of Bethlem Royal Hospital and Maudsley Hospital involved a patient who had a laminectomy (back operation) that led to partial paralysis. There was no question whether the surgery was performed competently, only of the failure to inform the patient that paralysis might result. The first court found that it was a "material risk" decision made for the defendant. "What degree of disclosure . . . is best calculated to assist a . . .

patient to make a rational choice . . . must primarily be a matter of clinical judgement." The British medico-legal orientation is concerned with the duties of the physician; it is a physician-oriented perspective. In America, the orientation medico-legally is concerned with patients' rights; it is based on a patient's perspective.

Why this seeming digression into law and systems of medical care? Because society in England currently limits choices for the bulk of its citizens; all alternatives are not available. Therefore, consent could not be truly informed. To avoid the frustration (suffering) of knowing there is a remedy but not being able to obtain it because of financial limitations, the patient's options remain undisclosed. The physician avoids telling an unpleasant truth, and this makes the physician an agent of the rationing power, as long as he or she fails to tell the truth, for it does not allow the patient to protest against a system with which the patient may not agree.

This raises further questions: Should a distinction be made between a physician's ethic and a medical ethic? (I have been speaking of them as the same.) Can a physician's ethic differ substantially from the imperatives of the society in which he practices? Is the idea that an individual patient's interests may differ from those of the society a reasonable position? Certainly, examples are plentiful: one-child population control in China; no-dialysis-when-you-are-over-55 in England; pushing to get Medicare patients out of hospitals earlier, in the view of cost constraints, in the United States; confining political dissidents in mental institutions in Russia. Indeed, in any state where physicians are used as agents of the society, there can be a conflict. Society as a whole must decide whether it is to its advantage to make physicians agents of the state (as illustrated in the Soviet Oath of 1971), or whether physicans should be patients' advocates. It is better for all of a society that its members never need to be concerned that their physicians are weighing their social value before prescribing, deciding whether they are worthy of the outlay of resources the doctor may recommend. Some other branch of society can be appointed to limit care on an economic basis or for other social imperatives, but the physician should never be the financial gatekeeper for society, should never disguise a social or political decision as a medical decision. It is incompatible with the physician's position as patient advocate, and threatens the trust that is so much a part of healing.

This, of course, has significant implications for the American system, as resources appear more limited and increased rationing looms on the horizon. Currently, about 15 percent of our citizens are rationed out of the system by our marketplace methods. Is our American unpleasant truth to be found in the Gordian knot of how to allocate resources; will part of the knife that cuts that knot be a limitation of access to medical care?

## Autonomy, Consent, Suffering, and Dying

A "Living Will" law failed to pass the Colorado Legislature for several years as a bill supporting patient autonomy, but it gathered sufficient legislative support when it was presented as part of a cost-containment package. This appears to be another example of doing the right thing for the wrong reason. Common-law rulings, which might be metaphorically described as crystalized ethics, have recognized that in the interest of self-determination, a patient must consent to therapy before it is administered (as illustrated above in the Schloendoff case). A necessary corollary must be the right to refuse therapy, even life-saving therapy. The landmark case in 1978 was Lane v. Candura. An elderly woman, who on occasion appeared disoriented and sometimes appeared perfectly competent, had a gangrenous leg. She was advised to have it amputated as a life-saving measure. She refused; she was taken to court by her son. The judge pointed out that neither the son nor the physician questioned her competence to consent to the operation, and therefore the judge questioned why they thought she was incompetent to refuse it. He pointed out that the physician and family were confusing competency with values. It appeared the patient was able to understand the consequences of her decision. Although she may have made a medically unwise decision, it was a question of whose values were to be honored. The case was settled in her favor.

The question that continues at issue is, "How far can self-determination go?" The morality that helps us answer derives from a variety of theological and other roots. There are similarities between Orthodox Jewish and Catholic traditions, in that both feel that life is inviolable, of infinite worth, and must be preserved. An Orthodox Jew says that saving one minute of life is the same as saving a lifetime. Both traditions indicate that life is a gift from God; the person is simply a custodian or steward and may not dispose of life, since it is not his or hers to dispose of. Jewish law treats pain and suffering as part of human fate; the reasons are yet a mystery. One may minimize pain and suffering, but it must be accepted. One must also consider that it might be the result of sin or the means of atonement for sin, as well as a test of faith. The Catholic tradition sees humankind somewhat differently. It is original sin that causes death and suffering. Suffering is acceptable for salvation. This, of course, was exemplified by the Inquisition, which tormented the body for the sake of the soul, as well as in the ascetic traditions, where mortification of the body is in the interest of salvation.

Liberal Judaism and the Protestant tradition make the individual responsible for interpreting the Gospel. Here, there is more a covenantal relationship with the Deity, and this as interpreted in the light of love for God and fellow man. In the religious viewpoints, pain and suffering are regarded as evil generally, but they are not necessarily so. In order to heal, one has two choices: to remove pain and suffering; or to give them meaning. Even though a disease may be local, the whole person is involved in it, and his understanding of it and his goals in life are affected by the disease.

The other force in our culture is modern American secularism, which in seeking self-determination speaks of personal equality and patient rights. These rights have further been subdivided into rights of liberty (freedom from interference in activities) and entitlement rights (those things that a citizen has coming by virtue of his membership in the community). Most decision-makers in this milieu are consequentialists, basing decisions on outcomes or expected outcomes. They are antiauthoritarian and accept little on faith that offends their intuition. It is an ethic of acting in one's own self-interest, as long as no innocent person is harmed; of being fair; and, insofar as one's own life objectives are not seriously threatened, benefiting others. It has been characterized in an oversimplified single phrase as "enlightened self-interest."

How then do these origins square with issues of death and dying? We have discussed the value of truth-telling and the value of consent in diminishing suffering from feelings of uncertainty and helplessness. When the inevitable time to die arrives, patients often suffer from damage to their self-image and loss of human dignity; suffer from the thought of useless depletion of all their financial resources; and suffer because they do not wish to impose needless additional stress on their loved ones, or the undeserved guilt that family members feel if they stop short of doing "everything" for the patient.

Taking the step of truth-telling so that patients are aware of their situation, and adding the principle of consent, allows patients to control their death as they controlled their life. From the courts and legislatures recognizing these ethical assents came "Living Will" statutes and judgments, permitting patients or their proxies to refuse treatment that serves to prolong dying rather than preserve living. Clearly, there is an element of quality of life that enters such decisions, and there is controversy about it arising from cultural attitudes.

There are at least two positions on this question. One position considers quality-of-life issues irrelevant, holding that any medically indicated treatment, that is treatment that will have a medical benefit, must be given. The moribund may receive palliative treatment or nothing, but for the unconscious, "there is an obligation to save life." This, of course, arises from the theological premise that patients are caretakers of their bodies and their lives are not theirs to dispose of. If such patients go untreated there is the fear of developing a policy of active euthanasia for those not dying. On the other side, there are those who feel that despite a person's incalculable individual worth, simple vital processes are not *per se* valuable, and the "kind of life" that will be preserved is crucial. Thus, there is a clash, which changes the question from, "Are treatments valuable?" to, "Is the patient's life valuable?" Those who do not hold to the theological stewardship analogy feel that the patient is the best person to decide if his or her quality of life is acceptable.

Society, represented by the law, has slowly evolved to the point that a terminally ill person may be allowed to die if that is his or her autonomous choice, but there is reluctance to permit a person to elect death based on a quality-of-life decision when death is not clearly very close. There are gray areas now and especially in considering artificial feeding. The two sides of the argument can be oversimplified as representing either fear that helpless elderly people in nursing homes will be cruelly starved to death, or the contrary fear that if a person is demented, incontinent, bedridden, and refusing feeding, society will mandate that they be tied in place and fed by tube until some ailment that defies medical technology releases them from such travail. That this barrier is yielding is evidenced by the Bartling case, in which a man on a respirator opted that it be removed, knowing that this act would cause his death. There is also the case of the ex–college president in a nursing home, who, at age 85, opted not to eat and refused artificial feeding. A judge upheld his right, and he was permitted to die. A third case is that of Claire Conroy, in a demented condition with five serious illnesses, confined to a nursing home where she lay in bed in a fetal position and had to be fed by tube while she was restrained, since she pulled out the tube frequently. A court ruled that this tube should be omitted, since it appeared to cause more suffering than benefit.

These decisions revolve around three approaches to ethical decision-making: obligation; motivation; and consequences. Often we have made a moral distinction based on whether an activity involves an act or a failure to act. This hinges on obligation, the role we play in relation to each other, such as doctor, mother, friend, son, or daughter. When do you no longer have an obligation? When a person with whom you have had a relationship releases you from the obligation. For a physician, this may be actual dismissal by the patient, or it may be a *de facto* dismissal, the person being dead or vegetative and therefore no longer having any interests by which the physician is obligated.

Activities have been distinguished as ordinary or extraordinary. These distinctions hinge on consequences of actions. The origin of this terminology is in sixteenth-century Catholic tradition. At that time, as now, suicide was considered a mortal sin. If one were to refuse therapy that had a chance of saving one's life, could that be interpreted as suicide? Since amputation was done without anesthesia and under septic conditions, it was not only extraordinarily painful, but a patient's recovery was dubious. Patients refusing this treatment were absolved from the sin of suicide since it was so extraordinary. Thus, "ordinary" and "extraordinary" relate to the burden of treatment, not to its availability. For example, using antibiotics for a young healthy person with pneumonia would be ordinary, but for the terminal cancer patient with intractable pain, the same antibiotics might be considered extraordinary. Similarly, cardiopulmonary resuscitation (CPR) in a young healthy person with cardiac arrest from, let us say, an electric shock, would be ordinary and expected, but the use of CPR in a terminal cancer patient would be extraordinary. It is best to consider these issues relative to burden or benefit and do away with the ambiguous terminology of ordinary and extraordinary. The consequences are the fulcrum upon which decisions turn.

A third distinction has been attempted based on whether actions were direct or indirect. These involve motive. This idea also arises from Catholic theology—the principle of double effect. Since we cannot always predict the consequences of our actions, the actions that we do directly with good motives may have indirect undesirable consequences for which we are not held morally responsible. There have been conditions enumerated to test for the validity of actions under the principle of double effect:

1. The act is good or morally neutral
2. The intention is good, not evil; though an evil effect may follow, it is not sought
3. An evil act must not lead to the good act; that is, the same act must yield both results, good and evil
4. There must be a proportionality between the evil effect and the good effect

An example is the use of strong narcotic for pain for someone in a terminal stage of malignancy, despite the fact that we knowingly shorten life: (1) giving the narcotic for pain is morally neutral; (2) the intention is to relieve pain, not to shorten life, though that can be foreseen; (3) the same act (using the narcotic) produces both the good and bad effect; (4) relieving the pain is proportionate, when considered against an agonizingly painful life.

*Killing and Letting Die*

Is there truly a difference between the sometimes morally acceptable "letting die" and unacceptable killing? There are times, we all know, that from our duty to prevent suffering, a logical argument could be made for killing. But, for society as a whole as well as for doctors, there is fear that once the barrier is broken, there will be unjustifiable killing. This could come about through error, mindless abuse, incorrect application of regulations, or simply a loss of concern for the defenseless. This school of argument is called the "wedge argument" or the "slippery slope." Wedge arguments protect the status quo. They allege that current rules must not be broken or there will be serious consequences. The burden of proof is on those who wish to promote changes in the current rules. They must show a logical stopping place on the slope. What have some of the stopping places been? What arguments have been advanced as exceptions to the prohibition of killing?

Killing is justified in self-defense. Almost all societies agree that an aggressor may be resisted, even at the cost of life. This argument has sometimes been stretched even further. For example, the Orthodox Jew prohibits abortion except to save the mother's life. Interpretations of the law use the doctrine that an assassin may be attacked to prevent him from murdering. The fetus is identified as an assassin threatening the mother's life, and therefore the fetus may be destroyed.

Killing is justified when the victim is not a person. This has served as the basis for some arguments for abortion. There is no prohibition against killing a nonperson. Some have argued for a semantic solution to this problem, calling a fetus a person from the time of conception. Others have argued for a definition of personhood and the beginning of life, analogous to our definition of brain death. It is argued that the undeveloped fetus, who has no electrically demonstrable brain waves until seven weeks, is not truly alive and may be aborted, but thereafter should be considered a person and protected by law. This "status by definition" can clearly lead to serious abuse.

Killing may be justified when death is foreseen but not intended; thus motive is important. This reasoning is derived from the principle of double effect, which we have already discussed.

A person may make an informed request to be killed. On occasion, when death is in the patient's best interest, there are those who argue that a patient may be allowed to die but may not be killed. Under this limitation, society is not threatened by the breach of prohibitions against killing. Proponents of this view presuppose a moral difference between initiating a chain of events and not interrupting a chain of events that has already been started.

Utilitarians argue that the end result is the same. That is, a person is dead, whether he is killed or allowed to die; therefore there is no moral difference. In fact, and quite the opposite, they maintain that if death is desirable for a patient, then one fails in a duty by not actively causing death.

Although it is often argued that the obligation to refrain from killing no longer exists if a person were to absolve us from that obligation, there are several hazards. Under social pressure, we may actually be getting a resigned assent to death, rather than an informed request. We must be certain that the patient is not in a temporary depression, which later may lift, so that the patient would be grateful that we did not accede to the request. The patient may have made an unrealistic appraisal of the illness or new cures may be on the horizon. Finally, the patient may perceive he or she is a burden on others and request death under these circumstances.

It is acknowledged that society must deal differently in allowing private acts, in contrast to condoning public policy. Whereas some acts of killing can be justified, prudence dictates they must be very carefully constrained as a social practice because of grave risks of harm. How has society recognized exceptions as justifiable? Friends and relatives who have gone to trial for committing mercy killing have usually been acquitted on grounds of temporary insanity; that is, they have been acquitted on a legal basis. Others, though convicted, have been sentenced very lightly. Physicians, on the other hand, could not go unscathed if they were acquitted on grounds of temporary insanity. A patient would be leery about consulting a physician officially labeled as having an unstable mental state, and a board of medical examiners might have to revoke the license. Therefore, society has "forgiven" physicians on factual grounds. One physician, who injected air into the bloodstream of a patient, and another, who used potassium chloride, were acquitted of homicide on the basis of an uncertain cause of death.

### Empirical Objections to Dropping Barriers To Killing

Despite good rational stopping points, which are morally defensible, there are those who fear the slippery slope from their own empirical observations. On occasion, society has not acted ethically and has been unable to draw rational distinctions. It is too easy a slide from self-directed to society-directed killing. Finances and the new stresses on cost containment might cause society to make ill-considered decisions. The slippery-slope argument warrants that this type of behavior causes a general loss of respect for human life. For example, there is evidence that, in China, insistence on each couple having only one child has led to a significant increase in female infanticide. The ratio of male to female infants in rural China is close to nine to one. Permitting death too easily diverts society from trying to find better and more humane solutions to human problems, such as good homes for the handicapped, the elderly, or the retarded, or such institutions as the hospice, which have worked so well for those patients with terminal disease no longer disposed to try marginal therapy.

Logical arguments can be made for exceptions to the societal prohibition against killing, but empirical observations show that many societies lack the ability to operate logically, and, in the past, grave harms have resulted. Should killing ever be permitted in our society, it must never be initiated by anyone except the patient and never in the interest of anyone but the patient, as the patient judges his or her own interest.

## Conclusion

I have presented a medical ethic that demands a balance. The goal of healing must be balanced by the goal of preventing suffering. When this is interpreted in the light of our social system's emphasis on self-determination, it follows there must be truth-telling, consent, and a fiduciary relationship in which a person with superior technical knowledge uses it on behalf of another. The medical-ethical perspective on human suffering must actually begin from a patient's perspective. The patient seeks medical attention because he or she is suffering. Relief of this suffering must be as much a part of the physician's goal as is healing. Many times when it is not possible to heal, it is possible to relieve suffering.

CAROLE A. ANDERSON

# The Severely Physically Disabled:
# A Subjective Account of Suffering

In 1972, an editorial appeared, in the *Archives of Physical Medicine and Rehabilitation*, titled "A Bill of Rights for the Disabled." Based on the assumption that the physically disabled had been denied access to the same civil liberties and benefits of life enjoyed by the able-bodied, it called for equal access to health, education, employment, housing, civil rights, and special training and placement. It required that architectural barriers be eliminated and special transportation provided. It argued for income maintenance and more research to deal with the problems of disabling conditions. The next year, the U.S. Congress passed the Rehabilitation Act of 1973 that was, in the words of then-secretary Joseph Callifano, designed to "open a new world of opportunity for more then 35 million handicapped Americans—the blind, the deaf, persons confined to wheelchairs, the mentally retarded and those with other handicaps." Callifano went on to say:

> The 504 Regulation attacks the discrimination, the demeaning practices and the injustices that have inflicted the nation's handicapped citizens. It reflects the recognition of the congress that most handicapped persons can lead proud and productive lives despite their disabilities. It will usher in a new era of equality for handicapped individuals in which unfair barriers to self-sufficiency and decent treatment will begin to fall before the force of law (Fact Sheet, 1978, 1).

In 1975, the United Nations adopted a Declaration of the Rights of Disabled Persons, to be used as a frame of reference by all countries to protect the civil rights of the disabled. Insuring the rights of disabled persons was intended to promote their integra-

107

tion, as much as possible, into normal life. The UN proclaimed that the disabled have the right to human dignity and the same civil and political rights as the nondisabled. Society has a responsibility to institute measures to assist them in becoming as self-reliant as possible; to provide economic and social security congruent with a decent standard of living; to consider their special needs; to make it possible for them to live with their families and participate in all social and recreational activities; to protect them against exploitation.

These documents, developed at a point in our history when many different oppressed groups were struggling for full participation in the fabric of American life, are testimony to the devalued, discriminated, and prejudicial status of physically disabled persons. Were this not the case, there would not have been the need for such declarations, resolutions, and laws. However, throughout history and in every place, the disabled have felt either positive or negative discrimination (Safilios-Rothschild 1970; Burgdorf 1980; Weicker 1984). Discrimination, according to Safilios-Rothschild, consists of both the unwillingness to allow the disabled to participate in the entire range of occupational opportunities and the refusal to allow them to become integrated into the general society. This latter form of discrimination, the most serious, reflects a deep-rooted prejudice based on the fears and anxieties of the nondisabled. Visible physical handicaps generate fear and anxiety in non-disabled persons, frequently causing strained interaction (Davis 1964) that, when it is at its extreme, results in social isolation. Social isolation can range from a reluctance to interact to restricting disabled individuals to special places—disabled ghettos, if you will—where their only interaction is with other disabled persons.

The plight of the physically disabled is a fitting illustration of human suffering and affliction. By virtue of their disability, disabled individuals are forced to endure (i.e., suffer) both the direct effects of their personal and functional limitations and the indirect effects of a disabling condition that assigns to them a new, undesirable, stigmatized social role. Freidson (1965) defines physical disability as social deviance, in the sense that a handicap or disability is a deviation from what the disabled individual or others deem "normal." In social terms, this difference has an imputed meaning of *undesirable* difference. Visibly physically disabled persons violate social norms for physical beauty and integrity and are "reduced from a whole and usual person to a tainted, discounted one" (Goffman 1962, 5). In Goffman's terms, the individual is viewed as possessing a stigma; others (i.e., normals) believe them to be "not quite human." A physically disabled person experiences the pain of an inferior social role in much the same way as members of all oppressed groups experience the pain of social isolation and prejudice. In a recent article, Asch (1984) reviewed empirical work in the social psychology of disability and concluded that the physically disabled are still socially stigmatized. They have limited opportunities to participate in ordinary life.

This chapter is based on a study of a group of severely disabled individuals, who attempted, as far as possible, the "ordinary life." Their efforts illustrate a particular form of suffering: the individualistic/subjective or phenomenological. A group of disabled and abled-bodied individuals became aware of what they called the "plight" of young, disabled people living in a nursing home, "[v]irtually entrapped in a stagnating, paternalistic prison where civil rights were violated, medical care was poor and impersonal, and individual initiative and creativity were not only not fostered, they were virtually discouraged" (Atlantis Community Inc., 1). In response, the group created the Atlantis Community and sponsored two programs: group housing located in an urban, public-housing development; and a federally funded needs-assessment project, which would make policy recommendations to federal, state, and city officials. We will focus on the physically disabled who were living in the urban housing development, and their "ordinary life."

The setting is eight housing units leased by Atlantis from the city. Each unit was renovated to make it wheelchair accessible. Seven units housed two severely physically disabled people each. An eighth unit was an office and central gathering place for residents and staff. The housing development was located in the inner city in a lower socioeconomic neighborhood. In the words of the cofounder:

> So here we are trying to make a more independent lifestyle in the heart of a slum situation; where we have a high crime rate and a high rate of alienation between the police department and the residents. In one way we are baptizing our people into reality at its extreme, and, in another way, we are being told by society, "All that is due you is slum housing" (Anderson 1977, 31).

In my original research, I spoke with the two codirectors and founders of the project (one able-bodied, one not), residents of the housing project, and four physically disabled persons living in their own apartments, two of whom had moved from the housing project. Most of the interviewees had been severely disabled from birth, with a variety of congenital problems. The rest suffered from progressive, debilitating diseases or the sequelae of a traumatic incident. In addition to interviews, I engaged in participant observation; stationing myself in the office of the housing development—the central gathering place for the community—to observe informal interaction.

We will look first at the institutional life in the nursing home, then at the attempt to remedy that problem, and, finally, at the ordinary life achieved away from the institution.

## Institutional Life: The Nursing Home

Long-term care facilities are institutions designed to care for individuals with health problems that interfere with their ability to care for themselves. Typically, residents are older people, whose health problems stem from advancing age. Some residents are almost totally unable to manage the activities of daily living and require total care. Others need supervision and access to central services, such as meals, recreation, and health care. Clearly, this population differs significantly from the young and physically disabled. However, they do share at least one bond: the inability to live independently within the mainstream of society.

Goffman (1963, 4) describes such institutions as a nursing home as "total," "whose total character is symbolized by the barrier to social intercourse with the outside, and to departure that is often built right into the physical plan, i.e., locked doors, high walls, water, cliffs, and forests." Typically, individuals sleep, play, and work in different places with different people, under different authorities, and without any overall plan. A central feature of total institutions is the breakdown of these three phases of life, insofar as all aspects of life are conducted in the same place and under the same authority. In addition, each phase of a resident's life is carried on in the company of many other people, all defined as alike, all treated alike, and all required to do the same thing. Daily activities are tightly scheduled, at prearranged times and in a sequence governed by explicit norms and sanctions. Residents of total institutions are viewed as a group, rather than as individuals, and staff engage in a process of surveillance rather than guidance. Characteristically, there is social distance between the residents and the staff; in particular, information that flows from the staff to the residents is tightly controlled. Work activity, if present at all, is usually trivial and unrelated to the structure of work in the general society.

A first encounter with a nursing home may be shocking and depressing. Glen, suffering from a progressive neuromuscular disease, describes the nursing home he went to as multistoried, surrounded by a chain-link fence, with a guard posted at the front door. On his arrival, a social worker told him that he would "meet wonderful people" (Anderson 1977, 152). However, on his first day he got lost because it was impossible to distinguish one floor from the other. What he saw when he got off at the wrong floor was, in his words:

> people in wheelchairs, probably right outside their rooms. Their wheelchairs were right up against the wall and the people were sitting there going "blah, blah, blah." And I went down through this and thought I had *had* it; I am going completely nuts. I didn't see this before when I was on my floor. Somebody said, "Hey, you are on the wrong floor. These two floors are off limits to people." There was only one person on the fourth floor, and he said, "Get out of here before you lose your mind." And I thought he was crazy (Anderson 1977, 153).

Glen had gotten off on the floor that contained "the basket cases." His response was to look out the window and say to himself:

> Well, if I have to stay in this place, I am going out the window. But that probably wouldn't do me any good; I would probably . . . end up on the third floor. This one guy was the only one I talked with in [that] place. The rest of them couldn't even hold a conversation. Then, the social worker says, "Why don't you organize them?" I said, "How can I organize them when, for most of them, their only wish is to die?" (Anderson 1977, 153).

Nursing homes manage large numbers of people. In order

to do that efficiently, many rules and regulations are devised to govern the residents' daily lives. George, who had been institutionalized almost since birth, describes his life in the nursing home:

> They got certain times, you know: what time you have to get up, what time you eat breakfast, what time you eat dinner, and what time you eat supper. That's a lot of headache. Sometimes they get me up too early. I would want to go somewhere and they say, "No," because they have rules and regulations (Anderson 1977, 180).

Glen, reflecting on his regulated life in the nursing home, recalls:

> Your room is not your own. Anybody can walk in and out as they see fit. . . . [Y]ou can't sleep with your door shut. People walk in and do what they call bed checks; they shine a flashlight in your face. That's the truth, . . . I can still remember calling a nurse every name under the sun, and it never changed one bit. They would still come in and shine the flashlight in your face just to find out if you are sleeping I suppose. . . . [I]f you are in a hospital or nursing home, you're nothing but another piece of machinery. You don't have feelings or thoughts. . . . You can be completely ignored as another human being. I've seen it more in nurses in nursing homes. There must be a good reason for it, but I can't put my finger on it right now. . . . You get a person and throw them in a nursing home and they have nothing. They do not have an education, and after a while . . . are completely stripped of . . . humanity. . . . [I]f you are in an institution, the institution has to, because it's economically feasible for them to do so, make sure you are utterly dependent on them. You cause them less problems all the way around. It saves them money because they can hire less staff. So, that is why you feel less human: Because you are made to feel less human (Anderson 1977, 139, 140, 167).

Reflecting on his own experience, Glen recalled the difficulty of forgetting it and described himself as feeling utterly hopeless while there: "I wasn't in there for very long, but I went in there and thought there was nothing left for me. After awhile it goes through and through your head there is nothing left" (Anderson 1977, 167). He goes on to say that when he was approached to leave the nursing home, he was afraid; afraid because he had resigned himself to staying for the rest of his life.

> But, you know, I already accepted that I was going to stay in there the

rest of my life. When I went into a nursing home, I accepted that. I think this happens to a lot of people who go into nursing homes. Of course, the younger people still have dreams . . . and they have problems facing reality, but that is part of reality when you do go into a nursing home. Most people you see in a nursing home say, "Hospital, nursing home, morgue." This is one of their sayings, and it is true. That's the way it was (Anderson 1977, pp. 167–168).

The founders of Atlantis, representing the militant attitude, described nursing homes as "paternalistic prisons that entrap disabled young people, violating their civil rights, discouraging individual initiative and creativity and providing poor impersonal care" (Atlantis Community Inc. 1976). Believing this, they organized to provide alternatives. The first step was to attempt to change the policies and practices in one nursing home, in order to make life more reasonable and ordinary for the residents.

Wade and Glen, the cofounders of Atlantis, met in a nursing home where Glen was a resident and Wade an orderly. Wade had been heavily involved with the civil rights movement as a minister. He had become discouraged and dropped out of the ministry to be an orderly, "and then," he said, "I learned my perception as a minister in a nursing home and as an orderly in a nursing home were two different games. I saw things very differently. And one of the things I became involved in was patient's rights. They had none" (Anderson 1977, 116). After working a short time as an orderly, Wade became "burned out" (Anderson 1977, 117) and accepted a job as an administrator in another nursing home. He hired Glen to work with him to try to create a youth wing, with policies that would be more appropriate for the young physically disabled residents. They accomplished many things and implemented a variety of youth-oriented activities, such as rock concerts and camp-outs. However, at some point the changes they were making became intolerable to the people who controlled the system. Wade says:

Well, then the polarization began, and the nurses on the other wings—the geriatric wing—felt the youth wing was getting too permissive. People were allowed to drink wine and beer, people were allowed to have sex: All those "bad things" we all do. So the clamps started coming down on our heads. I was called into the office to answer for some kind of thing that I usually found out was totally blown out of perspective . . . so I took a leave of absence. It got to me after a while. And Glen went with me, and while we were gone my whole staff was terminated. The custodial-mentality people were put in charge" (Anderson 1977, 119–120).

Wade and Glen never did return to their jobs in the nursing home; instead, they then set out to establish an alternative—a group living situation in the community.

## Community Living

Initially, Wade and Glen built a political base with elected officials who supported social-welfare reforms. These officials were later called to assist in expediting business with various governmental agencies. To bring their dream to reality, much hard work was needed: securing funding from the local and federal governments for remodeling buildings; working to change a system that did not have a mechanism to fund people living outside institutions; and securing the necessary resources to begin a training program. All of this was accomplished through many hours of raising funds, giving speeches, writing grants, and engaging in political activism. Wade and Glen also relied heavily on volunteers throughout the planning process. Eventually, the housing units were ready for the first residents.

According to Glen, the fourteen residents

did have some problems with the people in the neighborhood. I think they mainly saw us as some kind of threat. But now we receive compliments from them, . . . for instance, "Thank you for the stop light out there. Children were killed out here." We did get the curbs lowered, so it does help some of the elderly and those that go up to the medical clinic, which is a few blocks away. . . . we did help somewhat in that. There [were] things like theft. . . . [O]ne time a bullet came through one of the apartment windows and plowed [into] a picture of Janis Joplin. . . . [I]t wasn't aimed at us. It was just one of those nights when people were feeling their oats or something and someone fired a shot at someone. On the whole, I think we were treated very, very well. . . . [A]fter one instance, where some person who was partially drunk went into Susan's apartment and took a six-pack from her refrigerator, we called the police and had him arrested. It seemed like we were going to have a riot here, so we went around from neighbor to neighbor just telling them, "How would you like it if someone walked into your house and opened your refrigerator and took out some beer and told you to go to?" They seemed to understand it, and the charges were dropped and that was the end of any kind of incident (Anderson 1977, 136).

In spite of the general excitement about having reached their goal, there were still many problems. Wade recalls:

The only way we survived was by begging for money again, like we did in the nursing home. But, the residents have developed here in spite of the detriment of being in a slum situation. Some people say I overstate the case. It is a nice layout, in terms of the apartments being spread over 100 yards. In order for a resident to see another resident, he has to get out in the open air and see other people—able-bodied people as well as disabled—and interact in the community. And that is nice. This could be everything from a dream come true to a slum situation. It's all in how you want to view this. Some days I come in here and I think it's a slum. It's public housing, built in the forties, [and] the city doesn't give a damn if you tear them up or not. . . .[T]hey are going to put in ramps. They don't care because they're going to tear them down, anyway, in five or ten years. So, go ahead and use them (Anderson 1977, 120).

The young people who moved into the housing project were frightened, but they were independent. Moving meant different things to each of them, but central to all was the theme of control over their own lives:

To oversimplify it, it is a sort of giving everybody a right to independent living. That is a simplification, but that is the essence. Basically, I think that is what we're into, . . . just trying to make a person believe in themselves as a person, that they are another human being. This is one of the hardest things to get across to people: That we are people and why do we have to be put into a category?

We kind of feel like we're one big family.

My life is just beginning, which is strange, since I'm 34 years old.

It's not like a nursing home. It's more like being yourself. Being with other people.

To me, it's watching. It's not just watching people, it's watching others and helping others as others would help others.

It's a beautiful thing. . . . [W]e can make our own judgments; form our own opinions on things. We don't have to answer to some administrator in a nursing home. We don't have to kiss people's ass. We're free of that (Anderson 1977, 166, 187, 191, 197–198, 224, 216).

Being in a neighborhood community in the center of a city meant that the residents were not in a special place away from the general population, with access only to others similar to themselves. Rather, the ordinary, taken-for-granted facts and features of city life—usual persons, usual situations, and usual activities—were accessible. It was a usual place, made to produce usual, rather than institutional, routines. Being in a usual place was a major determinant of the life achieved by Atlantis residents, and their activities derived from and reflected their location.

Living among ordinary people requires the disabled to conduct themselves, as much as possible, in conventional ways. Their behavior must not stand out as being too different or they run the risk of negative sanctions and possible social exclusion. Atlantis residents tried to make their lives like everybody else's: by going to school, working, and, in general, conducting themselves in standard ways.

The freedom to lead conventional lives was a major topic in their accounts. Although desired and desirable, this freedom was also initially frightening. Glen described how, for example, residents frequently became physically ill when they first moved to Atlantis. In his opinion, these illnesses were prompted by a fear of being free; by the loss of the dependent relationship with the institution. They were unprepared for the responsibilities that accompany freedom; knowledge was needed to replace the absent constraints. The theme of freedom is reflected in the words of the residents:

Here you have freedom. I can really get out my feelings. And at the nursing home, I was afraid to tell anyone my problems.

Well, I think there has been freedom to develop and find myself. I think this is a perfect atmosphere. You are free to do what you can on your own, yet when you ask for help, even when they think you can do it, you're not nagged about it. So you can live more like a person.

I would call it probably a place where disabled people are free to develop and to get themselves to the point where they can contribute. That's what it's done for me.

One of the most striking things for me is the freedom from guilt. Even in the nursing home, we were different from the old people, and no one really wanted us around (Anderson 1977, 214, 189, 184).

Atlantis did not set up institutional rules or regulations to govern behavior. The residents were responsible for their own acts, were in charge of their own lives. They were able to act on their own wishes, realize their own ambitions, feel and do what they desired. The community was a source of support for them but did not exercise any control over their chosen way of life. They had become autonomous:

Well, the whole thing—in the nursing home you have so much dependency. You're dependent on everybody else to do things for you. When you move in here, it's like, I suppose, the first time you move away from home. That's the best way I can put it. When you move away from home you feel sort of alone—afraid—and don't have this warmth and dependency that you had upon your parents. You're out on your own and have to do everything for yourself. So, that's what happened here.

They want to go out by themselves . . . well, nobody tells them what they can or cannot do (Anderson 1977, 138, 157).

At Atlantis, people saw themselves as living individuated lives. In the beginning, this was difficult for some. Since many residents had never learned (or had unlearned) the skills necessary to conduct their own affairs, learning became a feature of their lives—learning how to negotiate the complexities of daily living. They had to learn about earning and spending money; how to budget and keep their checking accounts. Initially, many of the residents spent all their money when their checks arrived and, consequently, did not have enough to last until the next check. In the institution, the amount of money over which they had control was so small that money management was not an issue.

So they never knew how to write a check or keep a balance. It's the first time they ever had money because of how we had it set up. They would go on spending sprees and then they would find out, well, they didn't have any money left and the month still had three weeks to go. They would blow $60 in the first week. So they're slowly learning how to budget their money (Anderson 1977, 138–139).

Learning how to express human emotion was also slow. According to Glen, the necessity of having to be dependent on someone else, as a severely disabled person is, is linked to a reluctance to express anger and other emotions. In his opinion, a physically disabled person who is dependent on someone else for survival suppresses emotional expression. This suppression is, most likely, quite functional for the institutionalized individual. However, continually suppressing emotion in the face of the various provocative events of daily living may prove disadvantageous. Residents had to learn appropriate ways to express emotions. Glen comments:

Disabled people do get angry just like anybody else, but we suppress our anger, I think, ten times more. You were in nursing. How often have you really seen a disabled person really get super-angry, compared to able-bodied? Now I'm talking about a disabled person that needs the . . . able-bodied person . . . to survive. Do you understand?

All your emotions are suppressed. And maybe it's part of your anger, too. I mean, other people have anger, and they'll express it. I've seen disabled people trying to express themselves with a group of able-bodied, and I found out that able-bodied people will sort of gang up on that person. I've seen it in some of our meetings (Anderson 1977, 140–141).

Living with other people in an institution allows little opportunity to be alone. At Atlantis, however, there was privacy—a valued feature of the life for many residents. Privacy can also contribute to the development of sexual relationships. Although the lack of privacy in an institution is not the only constraint on sexual activity, it is a contributing factor. Atlantis residents began to develop an awareness of their sexual selves and were beginning to establish relationships:

[L]iving in the nursing home, you're not supposed to love another human being, and as far as sex goes, boy, they go right up [to] the ceiling about that. Naturally, no sex is allowed, period. . . . That's something else you have to suppress. I thought—that was another thing—I thought, "Boy, they're going to move out and what, they're going to go bananas." But, it's been the reverse. They don't. It's still suppressed, but it's getting more and more open. I can see it now: more and more free exchange and things like that. It's slow building up. I supposed it's sort of like an eleven-year-old testing out, and pretty soon they're going to be thirteen, but they're a little bit on the leery side, scared side, whatever. So it's going to be a slow process (Anderson 1977, 142).

Several Atlantis residents moved away from the housing project into their own apartments and further changed their lives. At Atlantis, they had acquired information and skills they needed for more independent living. Atlantis was a rehearsal. Although Atlantis was, in its own way, protective and isolating, it seemed to be an essential step for many who might not have been able to move directly into the community from the nursing home. Although they lived in a nonsegregated environment, there were still barriers keeping them apart from much of the world known to more ordinary people, such as having to be dependent on another.

## Dependence and Vulnerability

Assistance from an able-bodied person was still required to accomplish ordinary things that more able-bodied persons are able to do for themselves. Mobile attendants visited each person twice a day to cook, clean, do dishes and laundry, dress, bathe, make and change beds, shampoo hair, and do catheter care. Specific duties for attendants differed according to the abilities of the disabled person in the household. At first glance, this seems like a fairly straightforward matter, but on closer examination there was some evidence of strain in the social bond between the attendant and the disabled person.

Glen typified disabled people's reluctance to ask others to do things for them but was unable to explain why he thought them to be more reticent than the able-bodied. The norms of self-reliance and egalitarianism in our culture prompt people to want to do things for themselves and to be reluctant to ask for help or be served by others. Glen said he was reluctant to put another person in the position of being responsible for his survival. Although doctors and nurses knowingly and readily seek out and assume this responsibility, they are equipped with a cognitive body of knowledge and a set of norms and legitimized role behaviors with which to guide their actions. Because the Atlantis program was new, the home-care attendants lacked guidelines and, therefore, had to depend on their informal relationships with the disabled to guide performance.

A potentially troublesome situation can occur when the relationship between the disabled person and an attendant becomes a friendship. Accordingly, special effort was exerted to diminish the opportunity for friendships to develop. For example, attendants were rotated so that they did not always serve the same person. In this way, it was hoped that the disabled person would not prevail on the attendant to do special things that might result in the attendant feeling more was being given to the situation than warranted by, for example, the monetary compensation. And yet, the disabled person's need for friends and the attendant's compassion militate against maintaining a formal business relationship.

Each day in the life of the severely disabled person living in the community was characterized by attempts to transcend physical and social barriers. They were living in a world managed by and for the able-bodied. Mobility and accessibility are taken for granted by most able-bodied. Since disabled people's mobility is severely limited, they cannot take it for granted and must give extra thought and planning to ways of getting around to do desired things.

Unless disabled people are transported, they must stay within a short distance of their residence. Specially equipped buses frequently do not run at night or on Sunday and must be reserved well ahead of time. People with electric wheelchairs can go short distances; however, this mode of travel is hazardous. They must go on the street, since in most communities sidewalks are not ramped. For many, night life is limited to what can be done at home, such as watching television.

Although federal guidelines demand that old buildings be modified and new buildings accommodate the disabled, changes are slow in coming. Often, disabled people get away from home only to find that they cannot get into an unramped building and must be carried into it. Some of those I spoke with had registered and wanted to vote for the first time. Their polling place had thirteen steps to climb, so they had to be carried up or forfeit their right to vote.

Living in the community, the severely physically disabled were also constantly confronted with barriers to social interaction. Generally, this is a function of some combination of a lack of social skills in people who have spent most of their lives in institutions, and the discomfort of able-bodied persons who have not had an opportunity to develop an easy ability to relate to the disabled. The severity of their physical disability often makes it impossible to "pass" or "cover" and, at least initially, can be a focal point of any social encounter. Also, severely disabled persons occupy a marginal position in the social structure, which influences the nature of their interaction. They are without clear role expectations; as one resident said: "Right now I think maybe we don't have a role because the mere fact that people can grow up from childhood in an institution and in nursing homes, and the schools assign handicapped to special schools which really . . . the special schools really play down the need for education. I'm really not sure we have a role" (Anderson 1977, 85). If a role is assigned to them, it is, as Glen so forcefully stated when asked about the assigned social role, a devalued one.

> Okay, a mentally retarded nigger. I use the word "nigger," not black or negro or colored: That's the kind of role society has hung on us. . . . [T]oday we were at this press conference—I'm chairman of the board of Atlantis—so how do people treat me? By patting me on the shoulder. I've watched the same individuals . . . Some of these people . . . I'm their boss, they work in a different office but I am technically their boss, I can fire them if I want to. I watch them very closely, and I've never seen them place a hand on an able-bodied person's shoulder, just like a child, so I resent that very much. Sometimes I feel that I'm so angry that I'm just going to blast them out of their shoes if they put their hand on me again (Anderson 1977, 64).

Consequently, the severely disabled are excluded from groups of able-bodied and the less disabled.

Although opportunity existed in the community for these disabled persons to develop relationships with able-bodied persons, there were still barriers to overcome. In the meantime, it was more comfortable to maintain relationships with another disabled person. "It's really difficult even to establish a relationship with any able-bodied" (Anderson 1977, 83).

Those who had moved from Atlantis had lost some of the protection of the institution and the group situation; they were vulnerable. More vulnerable perhaps than the able-bodied, because their opportunities to learn such things as suspicion, caution, and discretion had been limited. It is easier to learn about life slowly and gradually, as a child, than suddenly and, perhaps, traumatically, as an adult. Susan, disabled at birth, thought that the most important thing that parents of disabled children can do is allow their children to experience many things, though it is easier for parents to protect their children from the pain and frustration of attempting to do for themselves.

A physically disabled person who lives among the able-bodied is more vulnerable to social rejection. Institutional living isolates a person from instances of painful, day-to-day experiences such as Susan encountered. "Like two nights after I moved in I went to the drug store to get some shampoo. While I was gone, the attendant came and the neighbor met her and said, 'One of them got out.' " She laughed. "I don't know what she was told while she was growing up, but as of yet I haven't figured out a way to come close" (Anderson 1977, 82.) Segregated living allows disabled people to avoid such confrontations with their differences.

As knowledge increases, vulnerability decreases; not all disabled persons are equally vulnerable. For example, Judy, disabled as an adult, did not seem to be as vulnerable as the others, She had acquired knowledge and skills to negotiate the vicissitudes of daily living prior to her disability.

> Yes, I think there is probably quite a bit of difference. Like with me, you know I can relate with people on terms other than as a disabled person to an able-bodied person. I've got a lot of past experiences that a lot of these other people just never had. Like they have to be taught to keep house and do their own shopping and manage money and stuff. I've done all that. So I've had a career, a husband, children. I've traveled. I've got a base of communication (Anderson 1977, 76).

Physical disabilities limit spontaneity: Activities must be planned around abilities. Judy had to plan in the morning what she was going to have for dinner, so that the attendant could help prepare the ingredients needed later in the day. "I need some help . . . When my aides are here in the morning, they open up cans that I know I'll be using, and I have them do things like cut up onions; I can, but it's very, very difficult. I don't do a very good job. I get a lot on the floor" (Anderson 1977, 76). Each day must be carefully planned. Judy's disability often interferes with the ability to hurry in order to finish a task if time is running out. Careful planning allows her to accomplish things without becoming overwhelmed by too much or bored by too little.

In a world that moves fast the slow movements of the disabled are out of place. Susan said, "The truth is I'm ten times slower than everyone else. Like it's hard to teach myself to relax and watch TV or just to go outside to goof around" (Anderson 1977, 85). She was able to do many household chores but had to sacrifice other things, such as work or social life, in order to get them done. However, she still felt the urge to try to do everything herself, even though she knew that many able-bodied people hire household help. Self-reliance, highly valued in our society, is frequently over-exaggerated when a person becomes disabled.

## Conclusion

The aspects of the disabled life that I identified seemed to me to be the design of a very difficult existence. I wondered whether or not the difficulties encountered by the severely disabled living in the community could create nostalgia for past institutional life, in spite of all its drawbacks. My doubt prompted me to inquire if any of them ever yearned for it. In fact, Susan defined living as possessing worries and struggles: "From this, I never could go back to a nursing home, because the fact is all the worries and all that they're worth, for me makes life worth living, having to do these things" (Anderson 1977, 85).

These severely physically disabled people became more a part of society and engaged in activities of their own determination: quite ordinary and fitting. Their involvements, though ordinary, were being undertaken for the first time, a reflection of their previous social isolation. Many of the features of their lives are those of the general lot of people, but the impressive aspect of these accounts of ordinary activities was the joy and enthusiasm they expressed. For many of them, as Susan said, life was just beginning.

REFERENCES

Abramson, Arthur S., and Bernard Kutner. 1972. "A Bill of rights for the disabled," *Archives of physical medicine and rehabilitation* 53. (March 1972): 99–100.

Anderson, Carole. 1977. *All the troubles and all that they're worth: Accounts of physically disabled persons attempting the ordinary life.* Ph.D. diss. University of Colorado.

Asch, Adrienne. 1984. "The Experience of disability: A Challenge for psychology," *American psychologist* 39. (May 1984): 529–536.

Atlantis Community Inc. 1976. Brocuhure (untitled).

Bowker, John. 1970. *Problems of Suffering in the Religions of the World.* London: Cambridge University Press.

Burgdorf, Robert L., Jr. 1980. *The Legal rights of handicapped persons.* Baltimore, MD: Paul Brookes.

Davis, Fred. 1964. "Deviance disavowal: The Management of strained interaction by the visibly handicapped." In *The Other side,* ed. New York: Free Press of Glencoe. 119–137.

Dixon, Jane K. 1977. "Coping with prejudice: Attitudes of handicapped persons toward the handicapped," *Journal of chronic diseases* 30 (1977): 307–322.

*Fact Sheet.* 1978. Rehabilitation Act of 1973. Sec. 504, *Handicapped Persons.*

Freidson, Eliot. 1970. "Disability as social deviance." In *Sociology and rehabilitation,* ed. Marvin Sussman. American Sociological Association.

Goffman, Erving. 1963. *Asifums.* Englewood Cliffs, NJ: Prentice-Hall.

Liunch, Hanoch. 1982. "On the origins of negative attitudes toward people with disabilities," *Rehabilitation literature* 43, no. 11–12. (November–December, 1982): 338–346.

Marinelli, Robert P., and Arthur E. Dell Orto. 1977. *The Psychological and social impact of physical disability.* New York: Springer.

Rehabilitation Act of 1973. 1973. Public Law No. 93–11, 87. Stat. 357.

Rehabilitation Act Amendments. 1984. Public Law No. 98–221, 98. Stat. 17.

Safilios-Rothschild, Constantina. 1970. *The Sociology and social psychology of disability and rehabilitation.* New York: Random House.

Weicker, Lowel. 1984. "Defining liberty for handicapped America," *American psychologist* 5, 39, 518, 523.

Williams, Robert S., Jr. 1984. "Ability, disability, and rehabilitation: A Phenomenological description," *Journal of medicine and philosophy* 9: 93–112.

Wright, Beatrice A. 1960. *Physical disability: A Psychological approach.* New York: Harper and Row.

Zola, Irving K., ed. 1982. *Ordinary lives.* Cambridge and Watertown, MA: Apple-Wood Books.

# Human Caring and Suffering:
# A Subjective Model for Health Sciences

"The question [of suffering] has two sides," he said. "An Objective side, and a Subjective side. Which are we to take?"

"Take the Objective view first. . . . What do we know? . . . Do you mean to deny the Objective view, so far? Very well, then. . . . Now arguing in this way, from within outwards, what do we reach? We reach the Subjective view. I defy you to controvert the Subjective view. Very well, then . . . what follows? The Objective-Subjective explanation follows, of course!" (Collins 1868)

Whether one starts with human suffering, or the humanities, or from philosophical questions about the nature of persons, caring, or health sciences, one ends up worrying about the same values—the enhancement, fulfillment, and enrichment of human life—the meaning one finds in one's existence. Mumford, in *The Myth of the Machine* (1970, 140), captured the general dilemma: "We must both in our thinking and our action come back to the human center; for it is there that our significant transformations begin and terminate." Thus, in proposing a framework of human caring for health sciences in dealing with suffering, the human center must be the starting point, before a significant transformation can occur.

It seems that one way to the human center comes from a deeper engagement in notions such as human caring and how we may better link humanities and human caring in understanding our human center—be it in suffering or joy. Caring, in this sense, is motivated by what Noddings (1984) calls "yearning for the good," in that human caring calls for a philosophy of moral commitment toward preserving and reintegrating humanity in the health-care system—a goal that is shared by art and humanities. However, while human caring may be motivated by a "yearning for the good," caring is not just an emotion, concern, or benevolent desire. Human caring involves values, a will, a commitment to care, knowledge, caring actions, and consequences. Caring is a serious, epistemic activity now pursued in the fields of nursing, health, and healing sciences.

Mayerhoff, in *On Caring* (1971, 13), remarks:

> We sometimes speak as if caring did not require knowledge, as if caring for someone, for example, were simply a matter of good intentions or warm regard. . . . To care for someone, I must know many things. I must know, for example, who the other is, what his powers and limitations are, what his needs are, what is conducive to his growth; I must know how to respond to his needs and what my own powers and limitations are.

But knowledge alone is not sufficient. Barnes (1985) suggests that human caring requires not only knowledge, but *wisdom beyond knowledge*. Wisdom from self can be imparted—the ability to learn from suffering and the ability to comprehend the subjective individual's life-world of suffering, as contrasted with the impersonal, objective world of medical science.

The subjectivity and wisdom beyond knowledge necessary for caring is likened to Prior's (1985) treatment of the concept of compassion, in that both caring and compassion are motivated by a sentiment, an emotion that Prior suggests is of central importance to morality, and that allows us to be touched by human suffering. Without such emotion, or subjective human response, something critical is missing in a caring relationship. Moreover, rationality alone can lead to suppression of the emotion of compassion, the motivation to reach out to the world of the one suffering. Such logical extension then can result in noncaring or apathy; one becomes detached, free, untouched by suffering. Noddings (1984, 8) associates such a detached state with the ethics of principles and justifications, versus an ethic of caring and responsibility. Noddings makes the further argument that caring is an inherent process that women use to approach moral problems, placing themselves as nearly as possible in concrete situations. They define themselves in terms of caring and work their way through moral problems from a position of one who cares. This process is inherent in nursing, a predominately female profession, gifted with caring.

Just as Prior argues that we should not put strict rationality before compassion, Noddings argues we should not put strict ethical principles before an ethic of caring for the person experiencing suffering in a concrete lived moment. Indeed, one definition of care is a state of mental suffering, in that to care means a stir of emotion, a call to the heart rather than the mind.

Therefore, caring as a moral ideal requires a process of concretization and an embeddedness in subjective human responses, so that compassion is stirred rather than abstraction, strict rationalism, and objectivity. Again, the nursing profession parallels the caring ethic, while the medical profession parallels the ethic of principles, rationalism, and objectivity.

Noddings points out that a caring ethic (toward suffering) is characteristically and essentially feminine. That is not to say it cannot be manifested by men, but it arises out of the feminine spirit in humans just as the moral-rationalist and traditional-logical approach to ethics arises more obviously from the masculine (medical) experience. Nursing, as a basically female profession, engaged in continuous caring processes and caring ethics, can more clearly illuminate suffering than can traditional medical ethics; i.e., nursing and human suffering call forth a model of human centeredness and subjectivity.

The objective-subjective dimensions need more exploration, however. Human caring requires attentiveness to the objectiveness of persons without reducing them to the moral status of objects. Gadow (1984) defined objectiveness as those aspects of the person that have been objectified, lifted out of the lived immediacy of the person's experience of suffering. The objectification has occurred either by the individual's own designation of a health condition, which includes personal suffering, or by application of a medical-science paradigm that abstracts the condition from the individual in order to address it as an instance of a disease or pathological category. Gadow developed this to say that both forms of objectification have as their end, if not the elimination of the condition (suffering), then the alleviation of the so-called pathological problematic aspects. Therapeutic efforts toward such forms of objectification by necessity address the objectness of person. However, to do so when the condition calls for objectification, while at the same time, and above all, protecting the so-called patient from being reduced to an object, is to engage in a professional caring relationship and to operate under a different paradigm than objective medical science.

As Gadow has pointed out, the forces of objective science operate in insidious ways to reduce persons to objects. One specific way by which persons are reduced to object status is to regard the body as a medical-science object. Such reduction negates the validity of the subjective meaning of the person's experience and inner life-world. Moreover, subjective meanings are categorically excluded in objective science. Clinical decisions thus are based on external interpretations, not on the internal meanings and coherence of the body, mind, and spirit as constituted by the person. As scientific object then, a physical body belongs to no particular person, for such objects have no subjectivity, no self, no suffering. In the worst-case scenario, the tension between object and subject occurs when, in the first case, *person* is reduced to *patient*; in the second case, *patient* is reduced to *body physical*; and in the third and worst case, *body* is reduced to *machine* (Gadow 1984).

## A Caring Paradigm for Health Sciences

The different paradigm that human caring and the humanities introduce in relation to suffering acknowledges and promotes inter-subjectivity and returns us to Mumford's "human center" in both the health professional and the person (so-called patient). It allows for human dimensions of suffering to be present in both the care provider and the care receiver. In turn, the intersubjective human flow from one to the other has the potential to allow the care giver to become the care receiver, receiving the awareness of suffering experienced by the other, and vice versa.

Some components of this different paradigm have been identified by Gaut (1983) who concluded, after her extensive philosophical analysis of caring, that the necessary and sufficient conditions for caring include: (1) awareness and knowledge about one's need for care; (2) intention to act and actions based on knowledge (wisdom, consistent with Mayerhoff and Barnes); and (3) positive change as a result of caring—judged *solely* on the basis of the welfare of others.

However, this so-called human caring, with its need for ethics, emotions, compassion, knowledge, wisdom, intentions, and so on, is always fragile and threatened because it requires a personal, social, moral, and spiritual engagement of self and a commitment to one*self* and to others' *self* and dignity (Watson 1985, 29). Human dignity, in this sense, is when one gives to self one's own meaning and so creates for self one's own integrity (Gadow 1984).

Human touch and human presence may in some ways directly and/or indirectly restore the human-centered subjectivity and dignity of both the care provider and the receiver of care. For example, in human touch, both subjectivity and objectivity exist. As Gadow puts it, subjectivity exists at the surface of the body. Touch is the dissolution of boundaries, be they objective or subjective. Touch offers the supreme risk in an individualistic society—the risk that one person's subjectivity (and I might add objectivity) will flow into another's. It is that very possibility, however, that makes it a means of overcoming the objectness to which persons are often reduced in health-care systems.

In the caring relationship, the body, mind, and spirit are regarded—and touched—often by the nurse (the feminine) as the immediate lived reality of the other person. Such action entails a breach of objectivity: empathetic "body, mind, and spirit" touch affirms, rather than ignores subjective significance. Its purpose is expression—an expression of the nurse's participation in the other's experience of suffering.

Because subjective involvement in another's suffering is possible only where caring, compassion, and concern exist, empathetic touch is concern made tangible. The caring relationship not only overcomes technology and objectivity by touching the self of the other, it also precludes a person's succumbing to the isolation of pure subjectivity—retreating totally into self. Touch affirms objectivity and subjectivity.

Sylvia Plath (1962), after her own hospitalization, captures both aspects in "Tulips."

The tulips are too excitable, it is winter here.
Look how white everything is, how quiet, how snowed-in.

I am learning peacefulness, lying by myself quietly.
As the light lies on these white walls, this bed, these hands.
I am nobody; I have nothing to do.
I have given my name and my day-clothes up to the nurses
And my history to the anesthetist and my body to surgeons.
They have propped my head between the pillow and the sheet cuff.
The nurses pass the way gulls pass inland in their white caps.
Doing things with their hands, one just the same as another.
My body is a pebble to them.
Now I have lost myself. I am sick of baggage—
I have let things slip, a thirty-year old cargo boat
Stubbornly hanging on to my name and address.
They have swabbed me clean of my loving associations.
Scared and bare on the green plastic-pillowed trolley.
I watched my tea-set, my bureaus of linen, my books
Sink out of sight, and the water went over my head.
I am a nun now, I have never been so pure.

Thus, objectivity and subjectivity can merge; the intersubjectivity of a caring relationship manifest in human "mind, body, and spirit" touch. Touch can reach past the objectivity of traditional rationalism, past the bureaucratic-technological system and scientific treatment, and past pure subjectivity, allowing the other in turn to reach out of the solitude of suffering, the place where each is living (Gadow 1984).

## Applying Humanities and Caring

Still another form of human touch occurs through creative imagination and development of new human-caring modalities and processes that systematically link human caring to humanities. The use of touch in this case is when the care provider allows for a human presence that can touch another's mind or spirit, and linger and remain, even in the physical absence of the care provider. As such, the aesthetics of caring through use of art, music, poetry, literature, and so on can become an extension of human presence and touch in the caring process (Updike 1985). Not only can the mind and spirit be touched through such modalities, but such approaches can potentiate healing and restore well-being.

Phyllis Updike's recent music research (1985) with intensive-care patients at the University of Colorado is an example of touching another with presence and sounds. She indicates that through music, boundaries between persons become similar to those of biologic membranes—a continual exchange of form, matter, and energy. The form of music may evoke specific feelings and release the person from self-absorption or suffering. Updike paraphrases Thomas (1983), who wrote, in *Late Night Thoughts on Listening to Mahler's Ninth Symphony*: "Biologic membranes are not *skins of cells,* but rather fluid matrices. Is not the very essence of art and music represented by its fluidity as it exists in space and time? And as we do too!" So in this way of thinking, the human center expressed through touch and presence, objective and subjective, responds with compassion and caring to the suffering of the other.

In the same sense, art and music are extensions of human life and a means of human-to-human contact. They are capable of touching another, in the absence of the caring provider, while still allowing human presence to be felt. Tolstoy (1896) describes art as the transmission of feelings. The activity of the arts is based on the fact that a person receiving another person's expression of feeling, through hearing, sight, or even intuition, is capable of experiencing the emotion that moved the other.

The link between human caring and the humanities strengthens if we begin seriously to consider how arts and humanities can be incorporated into new human-caring processes wherein the intersubjective mind, body, and spirit flow touches each self and unifies one with the other. I have referred to this potential human-to-human connectedness as transpersonal caring; each is touched by the human center of the other. To draw on Tolstoy's view of art, such an aesthetic caring process can begin when the care provider enters into the life space of another person (and vice versa) and is able to detect the other's condition (suffering). Through the use of self or aesthetic human extenders drawn from humanities, suffering can be felt by both; but the one who is cared for (with expanded aesthetic caring processes) can experience a release of subjective feelings and thoughts that had been longing and wishing to be released or expressed. This parallels Noddings' "cared-for" response.

Thus, both care provider and care receiver are coparticipants in caring; the release can potentiate self-healing and harmony in both. The release can also allow the one who is cared for to be the one who cares, through the reflection of the human condition that in turn nourishes the humanness of the care provider. In such connectedness, they both are capable of transcending self, time, and space. "In Whitehead's view, this shared caring experience can create its own field and become part of the larger, deeper, complex pattern of life" (Watson 1985, 59).

Dossey (1985, 204) captures this notion of mind, body, and spirit intersubjectivity and mutuality in his latest work, *Beyond Illness*. He asks, "What is the way out? The admission by the physician and the patient of the murky shadows within each—the woundedness of the healer and the latent healthiness of the patient." Such an admission would create the atmosphere for a new kind of intersubjective healing to take place. This intersubjective healing would truly be an alternative to the objective model of medicine as traditionally practiced.

Such an approach would entail no less than a radical transformation of traditional professional relationships. However, as intersubjectivity is allowed for, a new vision of the caring relationship begins to take shape, as both the care provider and care receiver become attuned to the two poles of their archetype (objective–subjective, masculine–feminine, compassion–rationality). The caring relationship transcends the traditional hierarchical stratification and goes beyond, so that neither care giver nor receiver stands above the other. (One might add, no one health profession stands above another.) In the new context, a basic humanism emerges in which the human centers of both persons are involved (both subjective caring and objective caring can coexist). Such an approach to caring leads to the affirmation of the subjectivity of persons that distinguishes them from objects. Thus, in a human-caring relationship—while the "object-ness" of the two may differ—the subjectivity of the care receiver is assumed to be as whole and as valid as that of the care giver.

Such intersubjectivity has been described by Buber (1965) as a dialog, as an I–Thou relatedness wherein the Thou is another human person. The relatedness is intrinsically different from the relation to an it or thing. Kant (1785) put it another way: Act always so as to treat humanity, whether in thine own person or in that of another, as an end-in-itself and not as a means. Thus, intersubjectivity is related to what Kierkegaard (1846) suggested as an existential paradox. It arises out of the dialectical nature of the genuine human self. To be committed to one's own existence is to be subjective; to be detached is to be objective. Again, Kierkegaard points out that a person must be both a subject (a center of commitment) and an object (an item of analysis). So, too, can the care giver be a receiver; so, too, can we find joy and suffering commingled.

According to Tillich (1952), to live one's life in the face of the demand, to "hold together" the ongoing tendencies is to engage in the dialectic of self-hood. So the objectivity and subjectivity of self is constituted as a synthesis of opposing tendencies that always remain in opposition but are held together by a "caring ethic," spirit or will, and compassion.

In *Concluding Unscientific Postscript*, Kierkegaard (1846) indicated that a genuine human being is a synthesis of the finite and the infinite and finds reality in holding these two factors together, but is infinitely interested in existence. The fact that suffering exists, then, is not necessarily a consequence of circumstances, but of the very nature of human life. Therefore, Dossey's notion of the wounded healer becomes grounded in the position that subjective suffering and mutuality (intersubjectivity) are moral foundations of human caring. The human center is restored and both care provider and recipient are prevented from being reduced to object status.

Rather than the logos of traditional medical science and traditional ethics paradigms—wherein suffering is viewed as a pathological problem that demands clinical therapy and distancing to achieve a cure—a caring paradigm, in the Kierkegaardian existential sense, views suffering as objectively and subjectively real and demands courage to reconstitute one's self. Each person is challenged to find meaning in his or her own existence. The existential problem of intersubjectivity is to be an individual self and be related to another's self. Neither challenge can be "solved" or cured; they can only be faced. Moreover, they cannot be made a completely rational, objective abstraction of principles and justifications; they demand an ethic of human-centered caring.

## Conclusion

Human caring and humanities can both be translated to subjectivity and intersubjectivity precisely because human caring and the humanities encompass subjectivity and expressivity and approach human existence—be it suffering or joy—from a reflective and internal (rather than external) frame of reference. A human-caring relationship then, by its very nature, calls for an ideal of intersubjectivity or an alliance with humanities. The subject matter of both human caring and the humanities comes from human life and the search for meaning, expressivity, and relatedness in human existence. The alternative to caring as intersubjectivity is not simply to reduce the patient to an object or means to rational medical science, but to reduce the care provider to that level as well (Gadow 1984).

To summarize, I quote from my book (Watson 1985, 59–60):

> An ideal of intersubjectivity (that incorporates subjective-self, human presence and touch and new aesthetic caring processes) is based upon a belief that we learn from each other how to be human by identifying ourselves with others or finding their dilemmas in ourselves. What we learn from others' condition is self-knowledge. The self we learn about or discover is every self; it is universal—the human self. We learn to recognize ourselves in others. The comparison shows us what we are, what humanness is, in general, and in particular, the intersubjectivity keeps alive our common humanity.

This returns us to our human center, so that from it transformation can come. Without the return to our human center and an ethic of caring, we are all reduced to objects. There is no hope without shared suffering or joy.

REFERENCES
Barnes, H. 1985. Unpublished presentation to the graduate seminar, University of Colorado Health Sciences Center, Denver.
Buber, M. 1958. *I and thou.* 2d ed. New York: Charles Scribner's Sons.
Collins, W. 1868. *The Moonstone.* Reprint ed. New York: Dodd, Mead, 1985.

Dossey, L. 1985. *Beyond illness: Discovering the experience of health.* East Lansing, MI: Shambahla.

Gadow, S. 1984. "Existential advocacy, technology, truth and touch." Paper presented to Research Seminar Series, University of Colorado Health Sciences Center, Denver.

Gaut, D. 1983. "Development of a theoretically adequate description of caring." *Western Journal of Nursing Research 5,* no. 4: 313–324.

Kant, I. 1785. *Groundwork of the metaphysics of morals.* New ed. Tr. and analysed by H. J. Patton. New York: Harper and Row, 1964.

Kierkegaard, S. 1846. *Concluding unscientific postscript.* New ed. Tr. Swenson, D. F., and W. Lowrie. Princeton, NJ: Princeton University Press, 1941.

Mayeroff, M. 1971. *On caring.* New York: Perennial Library; Harper and Row.

Mumford, L. 1970. *The Myth of the machine.* New York: Harcourt, Brace, Jovanovich.

Noddings, N. 1984. *Caring: A Feminine approach to ethics and moral education.* Berkeley: University of California Press.

Plath, S. 1965. *Ariel.* New York: Harper and Row.

Prior, W. 1985. *Compassion: A Critique of moral rationalism.* Paper presented at the Perspective on Human Suffering conference, University of Colorado, Denver. (Chapter 24 of this volume pp. 33–52).

Thomas, L. 1983. *Late night thoughts on listening to Mahler's Ninth Symphony.* New York: Viking Press.

Tillich, P. 1952. *The Courage to be.* New Haven, CT: Yale University Press.

Tolstoy, L. 1896. "What is art?" In *The writer's craft,* ed. J. Hershey. New York: Alfred Knopf, 1975.

Updike, P. 1985. Personal communication. University of Colorado Health Sciences Center, Denver.

Watson, J. 1979. *Nursing: The Philosophy and science of caring.* Boston: Little, Brown. Reprint ed. 1985, Boulder, CO: Colorado Associated University Press.

———. 1985. *Nursing: Human science and human care. A Theory of nursing.* Norwalk, CT: Appleton-Century-Crofts.